URBAN
ANIMALS

URBAN ANIMALS

a *comic* field guide

MIREILLE SILCOFF

illustrations by kagan mcleod

ARCADE PUBLISHING
NEW YORK

FIRST U.S. EDITION 2008

Library of Congress Cataloging-in-Publication Data

Silcoff, Mireille.
  Urban animals : a comic field guide / Mireille Silcoff ; illustrations by Kagan McLeod. — 1st U.S. ed.
      p. cm.
  ISBN 978-1-55970-898-2 (alk. paper)
   1. Human behavior — Humor. 2. City and town life — Humor. I. McLeod, Kagan. II. Title.

  PN6231.H763S55 2008
  818'.602 — dc22   2008031191

Published in the United States by Arcade Publishing, Inc., New York
Distributed by Hachette Book Group USA

Visit our Web site at www.arcadepub.com

10 9 8 7 6 5 4 3 2 1

Designed by M&S, Toronto

EB

PRINTED IN THE UNITED STATES OF AMERICA

The number of human types is so restricted that we must constantly, wherever we may be, have the pleasure of seeing people we know.
— Marcel Proust

CONTENTS

PREFACE

He must have been about seventy years old, and he was always at my gym, no matter the hour. He wore disturbingly small Spandex shorts. He was strangely sinewy. He was on a first-name basis with all the trainers. He probably had hair plugs. He was, in no uncertain terms, The Old Guy at the Gym — the type you can find at health clubs across the country. Anyone who has submitted to the tortures of the modern gymnasium has probably seen this specimen. He was *notable*, just not yet *noted*.

It was with this character that, in 2003, a weekly illustrated newspaper column featuring these Urban Animals was born. Seeing The Old Guy at the Gym in print wasn't going to change your life, but something about it was oddly pleasing. There is a certain satisfaction in recognizing something that you never realized you had already recognized — and if you are reading about it in a book or a newspaper, the pleasure is compounded by knowing that someone else has seen it too. It's the same feeling you get when you hear some random song on the radio and find that somehow you know all the words. If a comic strip can claim something so lofty as a purpose, then that of these Urban Animals is that single second where you go, "Oh, I *know* someone like that!"

Hippies, yuppies — by the time the column began appearing, those categories felt outdated, and brand-land variants such as "early adopters" had fallen into overexposure too. But there were other — in the grand scheme, less major — "animals" that were ripe for tagging. There was that person who was obsessed with his local neighborhood: The Localist, the authenticity-fixated type hanging out at the Portuguese or Italian or Brazilian café, proud that he seldom leaves a ten-block radius, and equally espiable in Brooklyn as in London's East End or Montreal's Mile End. There was also that thirtysomething dad in the Bad Religion T-shirt, clutching desperately onto his youth, possibly still subscribing to snowboarding magazines, and expressing a little too much interest in his son's *Star Wars* figures. Or the woman who had gone over the top self-diagnosing phantom medical conditions on Google and Medline — a new, and altogether pervasive, kind of urban neurotic.

Luckily for all of us, the talented young newspaper illustrator Kagan McLeod signed on for the project of turning these animals into characters you can see, adding his remarkable wit to my often questionable humor. If Beastie Dad looks like someone you've noticed, it is a tribute to Kagan's knack for knowing exactly what kind of stickers such a type would have peeling off the side of his computer.

Both Kagan and I would like to send a massive rosy bouquet of thanks to Dianna Symonds, who was our first editor at the *National Post* and gave the column the green light and then saw it through its first year. Also to editors Sheilaugh McEvenue and Sarah Murdoch at the *Post* for dealing with a sometimes refractive sense of deadline. Thanks as well to Chris Bucci and Doug Pepper at McClelland & Stewart, and to my agent, Ira Silverberg. Also to Michael Kronish, Jonathan Handel, Alana Klein, Rebecca Weinfeld, Jonathan Goldstein, Adam Sternbergh, and Sarmishta Subramanian, whose minds sprung a few of the animals you will find in the following pages.

I would also like to simultaneously express gratitude and apologize to a great number of my friends and my extended family, most pressingly my four parents, who may have found bits of themselves turned into an Urban Animal at one point or another. The day you all decide to get back at me is a day I hope I never see.

And thanks, of course, to the weekly readers of the column, a phenomenally loyal bunch. The hundreds of letters and suggestions you have sent in over the years are constant fuel for Kagan and me. When enjoying this book, please remember that a wicked cackle is what we've been going for all along. If said cackle arises, we've done our job well. And if you find yourself in here, consider yourself lovingly branded.

— Mireille Silcoff

BEASTIE DAD

AVERAGE AGE: 38
NATURAL HABITAT: Back office, skateboard/snowboard shop

Named his son Paul not after the apostle but after the "incredibly awesome and underrated" 1989 Beastie Boys album, *Paul's Boutique*. Knows he is the raddest dad ever. Not only can he get Xbox games before they come out (an old buddy from the Aspen days is now a designer at Microsoft), but at the skate park Beastie Dad's still able to pull a Backside Lipslide better than any of the kids. Was once the king of the ramps on the Vans Warped Tour, after all. But then Betty got pregnant, and Beastie Dad injured his hip after downing a bottle of Jägermeister and jumping off the balcony at that Bad Religion concert, so they opened a skateboard/snowboard shop, and, combined with some contract carpentry work, the settled-down-parenthood thing's turned out pretty cool. Is slightly worried that ten-year-old Paul's lately been saving allowance money to buy *The Most Relaxing Classical Music Album in the World . . . Ever! Volume 2*. Also, his son's "depression" over the last episode of *Frasier* was kind of weird. And what's up with this "Dad, could you *not* pick me up from chess club on your longboard" stuff all of a sudden? Since Paul got into that Brontosaurus school ("Montessori, Dad"), everything's changed. Betty says Paul will come around again, and, until snowboard season starts, Beastie Dad will have to go to the skate park without his little buddy. ("*Nobody* thinks you're too old, honey. If it makes you feel better, you can say it's research for the store.")

THE SOCIAL SMOKER

AVERAGE AGE: 35
NATURAL HABITAT: Bar patio

Can't believe she used to smoke a carton a week in her twenties. Now The Social Smoker can go for *days* without smoking — really, it's no trouble at all. The SS only smokes when she is out at night in appropriately drinky situations. Lately, she's been out a lot, not that it's becoming a problem or anything. Although she did have one Parliament when she was writing that impossible report yesterday afternoon, but that was just for concentration, and she had one when visiting old puffer Aunt Suzie earlier today, but it was more for Aunt Suzie's sake than anything, and then there was last weekend in New York, but in New York *everybody* smokes, so it's not even really like smoking, it's just "when in Rome." Feels sad for those pathetic addicts hanging outside their offices at lunchtime in the rain — different, of course, from hanging outside bars and restaurants at night. "You meet the most *interesting* people outside," she says. "It's like a little private club." Makes a point of not buying her own cigarettes, because, well, she smokes so little that they would just go stale, wouldn't they? Knows that the people outside don't mind when she bums, because she does it in this really cute way ("Hi, guys, I know this is sooo annoying, but . . ."), and anyway, they're all in it together! The al fresco crew! The ones who really know how to have a good time! Got a little bit worried when she bummed an extra one the other night and wrapped it in a napkin to bring home "just in case." Blowing smoke out her apartment window at one in the morning, the SS decided that next week there'll be no going out, only DVDs and chips on the sofa. That should get everything back on track.

THE BELATED PARTYER

AVERAGE AGE: 35
NATURAL HABITAT: Middle of the dance floor

It's not that The Belated Partyer's early years were understimulating. From law school to business school to the job at the big firm, it just never occurred to him that he "was not really living." It took being laid off for him to see it. "Fourteen-hour days and all-nighters at the office? For what? Working more to buy more?" He had "the big epiphany" when his friend Jeremy's little sister invited him to her birthday party, which ended up at an after-hours club. "Saw the light on the dance floor"— a glow enhanced by some fascinating chemicals. "You know, these DJs are more like magicians than musicians!" he told Jeremy's sister as he unbuttoned his sweat-soaked Thomas Pink shirt. "They know how to get straight into the mind!" He used to go hiking for fun on weekends, and "partying" meant drinks at the banker's bar —"frat life, but with cash and sashimi." Now it's all-night dance-floor madness and "hardcore mixing" on his Technics 1200 turntables, which he has installed in his bedroom. None of his old friends are into his new "lifestyle." He took Jeremy to see Armand Van Helden "spin," and Jeremy told him he still preferred "a good bottle of shiraz at a raw bar." Now the BP's coterie is made up of twenty-four-year-old bartender hotties, and the bouncers at the clubs let him in with no wait. He ran into Jeremy's sister the other day at Blockbuster when he was renting *24 Hour Party People*. She looked at his Adidas track pants and diagonally slung messenger bag. He asked her to go with him to "the big DJ Hell thing" on the weekend. "Oh my God!" she said. "This is so cute! You're like a raver but twelve years too late!" Has just bought a vintage Moog synth and has sent his "tracks" to some guy he met from Ninja Tune records. Still has not heard back.

THE YOGIC LAWYER

AVERAGE AGE: 57
NATURAL HABITAT: Executive yoga class

Was once "dead inside" but is now capable of "natural high." Never knew how comfortable a drawstring on trousers could be. Trying to figure out how to imbue corporate environment with some of the Eastern spiritual wisdom gleaned from Ashtanga. Might have a small Buddha sculpture or shallow vase featuring smooth rocks and bamboo shoots on office desk. Plays whale music while writing memos on titanium laptop. Now takes wife (unenlightened: does Pilates) on trips to rural Thailand for Christmas, instead of St. Barts or Zermatt. Recently dropped half a cranberry Clif Bar on the floor and actually picked it up and ate it (bacteria can be good for the immune system — what are we but earth ourselves?). Felt only slightly ill that evening. Will *not* fantasize *anymore* about having affair with fragrant instructor at Bikram studio.

MISS HAPPENSTANCE

AVERAGE AGE: 29
NATURAL HABITAT: "Oh, wherever . . ."

The worst kind of contemporary style snob, the human version of distressed denim, Miss Happenstance says she is a "fluke magnet," and she would like for you to think so too. She's the one who always has the perfectly worn T-shirts and the brown leather boots that never look too new but always just right. Visible makeup and any other sign of effort are anathema to her loose, slapdash style. That solid-pine butcher-block table in her kitchen? "Yeah. I just found it in a Dumpster." The vintage Yves Saint Laurent blouse? "I dunno, it was just lying around my mom's house." Her messy pieced-out hair? Miss Happenstance waves off coiffure-related compliments with an "I just, like, cut it myself whenever it gets too long. I always forget to put conditioner in." Miss Happenstance would also like you to believe that the stack of books and magazines by her toilet are just random (maybe she *does* read Thomas Mann on the can). And, given that she finds disagreeable anything that looks contrived, she would most certainly not like you to know that said pile was toiled over for an hour last week or that the *Us Weekly* is there to make the rest seem more believable. Miss Happenstance will just *happen* to be at a wide array of exclusive events. Wearing a seemingly random collection of bangles jangling on her wrist (a mismatch that took at least fifteen minutes to perfect) and no bra (bras are so uncool — everyone from Kate to Sienna knows that), she will claim that she has just popped in on her way someplace else. Women tend to be wary of Miss Happenstance. Men fall for her easy-breezy, tomboyish schtick like bowling pins. Ex-boyfriends, who have seen her manic flip side, are kept quiet by her deft use of precision-crafted blackmail.

THE SYCOPHANTIC WAITER

AVERAGE AGE: 28
NATURAL HABITAT: At your service

Just a milk-fed prairie boy, he moved to the big city when a modeling agent spotted him at T.G.I. Friday's in 1994. Was the eleventh guy to the right in the ck one ad in '95, but today his true vocation as a man of the stage has become something he can no longer ignore. Now that he's done that AT&T ad, he knows that his big acting break is just around the corner, or "maybe in the corner booth, sitting with that superconnected entertainment lawyer." Every table is an opportunity, that's what The Sycophantic Waiter always says, and so he's developed his own "wait style." Can drop a "coulis" or "reduction" with serious trill. And while some diners may seem perplexed when the SW offers them pepper in his signature way ("First-growth grains de Tellicherry, ground to order?"), they can't help but be impressed by his flourish. Of course, Chia Som, the chef at Chia, the hottest Franco-pan-Asian restaurant in town, is a genius (or "insane megalomaniac"). All of Chia's cherished regulars (or "moneybag suckers") like to think that, anyway. Little do they know the real genius in the house is the SW, who's even beaten lifelong waiter Silvio ("Lifelong loser, more like. He's *fifty-one*!") at convincing the lovely diners ("Can they even *chew* with all that Botox?") to "indulge" in the $150 tasting menu. "Oh, sir, a man of your connoisseurship deserves to experience Chia's whole range of exotic flavors. It is *only* for epicures such as yourself." If he's a bit rushed in "introducing" you to the Madagascar Vanilla–Infused Bison with Heritage Tomato and Microsprout Garnish, it's only because he just spotted Kim Cattrall — she's probably real cozy with casting people at HBO, and he's gotta get to her before that tip-slave Silvio does.

MS. 2000

AVERAGE AGE: 33
NATURAL HABITAT: Manhattan

She'd had New York on the brain since she was a child, so she moved there in her early twenties, during the dot-com boom. She never believed the technology bubble would burst, and when it did Ms. 2000 decided to stay, despite all that *annoying* talk of "scaling down for new economic and political realities." Through extreme effort, she has managed to continue living as a "fabulous chick," albeit increasingly deeply in debt, having decided that "what I really enjoy is a fine cocktail in an expensive pair of Manolos, creditors be damned!" The annoyance caused to friends by such statements is proof of Ms. 2000's peculiar limbo of outmodedness: the era in which she is trapped is old, but not old enough to be considered retro (and thus acceptably quaint) yet. Her friends have long left behind coked-out nights in strappy stilettos, opting instead for teahouses and "authenticity" in Brooklyn (they now call Manhattan "the banker's shopping mall over the bridge"). Even so, Ms. 2000 still only eats out in big restaurants in the Meatpacking District, where every piece of food is "stacked" and every piece of furniture is a variation on the cube. She drinks colored cocktails in martini glasses and prefers wearing pants (often white ones), both low-waisted and flared, with shoes resplendent with gold and logos. Her Fendi baguette purse contains condoms, a variety of bronzing powders, whichever credit card is not maxed out, and an address book with the numbers of a dwindling collection of "fuck buddies" (most of them have moved to Brooklyn too). Loves Jay-Z, *Wallpaper*★ magazine, and books by Sophie Kinsella. Her apartment in the Village is the size of a stamp and costs three thousand dollars a month, but, of course, Ms. 2000 maintains, "It's a small price to pay for living in the center of the universe."

DON GARMENTO

AVERAGE AGE: 36
NATURAL HABITAT: Los Angeles

Don Garmento did not come from a schmatte-business background. Father is a professor, mother a psychologist. At age fourteen, he shocked his forebears by selling knock-off Hilfiger T-shirts from the back of his dad's old BMW. As an undergrad, he ran a full-scale bootleg sports-team-cap business from his dorm and had a battalion of young lackeys shuttling cash and goods around for him. He repaid favors with FedEx packs stuffed with pot (which he never touched himself—"The brain of a man on a mission can't go soft"). His lackeys called him The Don — which, of course, he loved. Business exploded with the street-wear boom of the nineties. Relocated to Los Angeles and began specializing in cotton goods. Made his first million, he says with typical hyperbole, by initiating his "great tennis-sock revival." His second million was the result of his "halter revolution." "No one was doing halters back then. The market was creaming for halters." Has now gone "totally organic cotton," claiming it's "for the good of the planet" rather than the good of his ever-expanding empire, which today includes a slew of retail stores in gentrifying neighborhoods. Has a reputation for debauchery. Claims to have slept with four hundred women in the past two years alone ("no less than 50 percent Latinas") and enjoys putting sex references in the quotes he gives to magazines. Insists on writing his own ad copy. His most recent ad — currently found on the back of *Vice* and various free weeklies — features a photo of his own bare backside (shot by Terry Richardson) and the tagline "This ass wants to clothe yours. In organic cotton. The planet deserves it."

THE PLUS-SIZE MODEL

AVERAGE AGE: 21
NATURAL HABITAT: Side of a bus

The Plus-Size Model was just a regular model — living on white powder and the odd stick of Trident in a Tribeca loft with two bony Ukrainian teenagers — until she had her "Epiphana? Epiphanis? What's the word? When you, like, suddenly see everything clearly?" She had it last year, when she found that her dress size had shrunk to the point where even zero was baggy, while her agency was telling her she still had "haunches." "I'm less than zero!" she cried. "Like that scary eighties movie with the cocaine and the glamorous lifestyle that's not really glamorous." After the epiphany, she left her agency, didn't even say goodbye to Anasthasia and Oola, and went back to Mom and Dad, who fed her "at least two bagels" every day. Then she started eating "meals, actual meals. It was so crazy." She emerged "totally empowered, like Tyra Banks." Banks, of course, is the goddess of all haunchy models, being haunchy herself but still in Victoria's Secret ads. Now signed with Beautiful Curves — the agency that "lives largely" because "Beauty doesn't only come in small sizes" — the PSM is doing work for Talbots and Lane Bryant and not McQueen or Jacobs, but, as Oprah says, at least she is being "body true." She's now featured in a campaign for a "hip" clothing brand aimed at the size-twelve-and-over market, wearing leather and ripped denim and reclining languidly in a filthy South African coal mine. "Total grime-chic, for real women," says the PSM. The ads have gone on the sides of buses in seven major cities, which has sparked not a few "booty like the side of a bus" jokes on modeling industry Web sites. The PSM ignores them. After all, Anasthasia and Oola are now back in Kharp and Birobidzhan, respectively. "And me," says the PSM, "I'm on the *streets*."

THE SEASONED ROCK CRITIC

AVERAGE AGE: Too old
NATURAL HABITAT: Back of the venue

Will not go "the way of the yup-yup" and become a film reviewer like "all those minivan drivers" who once called themselves rock critics too. Started feeling like "the oldest guy at the venue" around 1994, "back when music magazines were more than download guides" and "real rock involved someone on speed hitting pigskin at the back of the stage, not a vegetarian pressing buttons ironically." Has now accepted that most kids at the shows think he's a narc. Has been wearing the same tapered black Levis and flattened Doc Martens for so long they have "lived out two cycles of revival. I had these boots when The Strokes were still in their Teenage Mutant Ninja Turtles phase." Has an ex-wife and a kid in New York. Used to spend a lot of time there when the review sections in the magazines "had a better understanding of true music" (see pigskin, etc.). Now gets one or two reviews a month if he's lucky, often a box set for the reissues column. Hates hip hop. Hates dance music. Hates "world beat," which he refuses to name as a genre without quotation marks. In the early nineties, was more into Archers of Loaf than Pixies, but recently went to the Pixies reunion show anyway. Got onto the guest list care of the music editor at the free weekly. "Go with Sheera," said the editor. "She's reviewing the show." Sheera? "Yeah, she usually covers DJ stuff, but I figured she'd have a fresh perspective." At the show, Sheera said she was "totally into" the SRC's "oeuvre." ("I'm *sooo* into anything eighties!") One of her friends said he was pleased to meet Sheera's "father." That night, the SRC went home and alphabetized CDs until four in the morning, concentrating on the film soundtrack shelves. Maybe a few movie reviews wouldn't hurt too badly.

CRAZY CELEBRITY (2005 Edition)

AVERAGE AGE: 27
NATURAL HABITAT: The tabloids

Was once "a buxom beauty" (code for "downright porky") before becoming "svelte" (read "deathly skeletal"). Was recently seen going into a fertility clinic in London ("the hot place to plan your baby!") but has no sign of a "bump" yet, though "insiders" say that the CC/05 has already "ordered three thousand gallons of Fiji water" to fill her Malibu swimming pool for an underwater delivery ("the hottest way to have your baby!"). But who is the loving father? The CC/05 has been "sending out mixed messages" through "cute cropped T-shirts," including the now classic "I'll have your baby, Brad" (she's since made a public apology to Jen — poor, poor Jen, jogging in the park all alone), and the more recent and infinitely dumber "Colin is Irish for Greek god." Some think the baby rumor is the CC/05 trying to divert attention from the obviously surgically amplified breast she bared "by accident" at the Golden Globes while obliterated on OxyContin and Bacardi Breezers (and only two weeks after her actor beau of three months was caught "heavily canoodling" with a nanny in St. Tropez). Denies any connection to Scientology. Denies she fired her manager because the Scientology center forced her to. Denies that maybe she had a little nip of Vicodin ("Drugs are in my past! Drugs are bad! Just say no!") before doing the "stirring the pot" dance on Oprah's sofa for a full minute after being asked how she's doing these days. Is photographed perplexingly often at gas stations, barefoot, carrying a large coffee beverage.

THE MOODIE

AVERAGE AGE: 40
NATURAL HABITAT: "On the culinary edge"

The Moodie is a specifically male kind of foodie, one who marries his culinary preoccupation with an in-your-face burly masculinity, partly to let the world know that, while he is most certainly a gourmet, he is *not gay*. To prove how not gay he is, The Moodie, who may be a chef, caterer, restaurant critic, or lifestyle-magazine editor, champions only the manliest of edibles and cuisines. His is a world of offal, smokehouses, slabs of meat, and "extreme eats," such as Asian pufferfish "that can kill you if not prepared properly." You won't find The Moodie in "the sort of joint"— The Moodie will often use words like *joint*— "where it's two bites of pastel-colored shit [the Moodie is also fond of profanity] on a plate where some kitchen fop has made a Jackson Pollock out of coulis" (the Moodie hates coulis, though he likes Jackson Pollock's "muscular" take on art). For The Moodie, "food is an adventure," and holidays can mean trolling Texas in search of the best barbecue or a trip to Bhutan in order to sample yak butter tea, a concoction that "more femme" foodies have called "the most disgusting beverage on earth." Other leisure activities include giving long, pretentious sermons about single-malt Scotch or pure blue agave tequila, womanizing (he's *so* not gay!), smoking (Marlboro Reds), working out (in a very not-gay way), doing the odd line, and squinting into the sun from behind the wheel of a '72 Mustang convertible while trying not to admire his profile in the rearview mirror.

THE CONDESCENDING VEGETARIAN

AVERAGE AGE: 32
NATURAL HABITAT: Vegan tea shop

Misses the nineties, when it was more acceptable to call a hamburger "evil" just as a dining companion was about to eat one. Now it's different, and meatless eaters like The Condescending Vegetarian find themselves mocked as being PC when voicing even the most casual disgust at the table. Recently rented *Super Size Me* and was dismayed to see "vegetarians as the joke-butt in even the anti-McDonald's movie." Sanctimonious by nature, the CV now tries to hold in her derision and has even been overheard saying she finds "those who critique the food choices of others just as annoying as anyone else does." She still can't help crinkling her nose at steak ("Me? Oh, nothing, no! I just have to sneeze") and finds the word *chicken* funny ("Well, it's just, you know, *bok-bok*. What — you don't think it's funny?"). The CV tries to keep mum in the presence of veal but lost it last week when her roommate brought home a massive chop. "Babies in cages! Babies in cages!" she wailed. The CV then left the house to have dinner at the vegan tea shop, the one with the rickety flea-market furniture, feminist art-show posters, and Peruvian wind music soundtrack. She ordered a tofurky sandwich and a lemongrass infusion from the young kerchiefed waitress, and then ordered another infusion after finishing the molded protein sandwich. "Drowning your sorrows?" asked the waitress. "I think," said the CV, "my roommate is secretly a neocon."

THE APPIE

AVERAGE AGE: 28
NATURAL HABITAT: "It's kind of like a commune, really."

In the pantheon of posthippie types (zippies, yippies, gippies), The Appie (apolitical hippie) has so far gone undocumented. To the casual observer, he may seem like standard-issue hippie, with his Guatemalan drawstring trousers, matted honky dreadlocks (sometimes tied in head-top ponytail with a bit of soiled fabric otherwise kept around wrist), propensity for remaining unwashed for days and for talking very slowly using words like *energy* (as in, "I was getting weird energy off that guy"). A closer look, however, reveals a different sort of species. The hippie is a type with a strong political underpinning. The Appie, on the other hand, takes pride in being completely clueless about current events. To The Appie, this ignorance signifies that he is on a "higher spiritual plane"; it's a two-fingered salute to the countless nefarious entities he views as "corporate." In his younger days, spent his summers as a tree planter, a Deadhead, or a follower of "jam bands." Now finds that many classic hippie mainstays (yoga, the green movement) have been "co-opted" by "mainstreamers." So The Appie carves out his identity by eating only brown foods (wild rice, molasses, miso, odd teas), meditating in public, "not being materialistic," and living in a house with many other people, including, preferably, at least one single mother who may or may not be studying tarot. Big on "freedom," "living light," and "self-expression." May carry a pan flute or devil sticks in his back pocket in case the need to self-express strikes. Did not vote in the last two elections, he says, not because of self-absorption but because the political parties are all "too corporate."

THE LOCALIST

AVERAGE AGE: 25
NATURAL HABITAT: Gentrifying urban neighborhood

Has not left a ten-block radius in eighteen months. Prides himself on not going anywhere he can't walk. Why would he? The neighborhood provides everything The Localist needs. As he always says, "There's nothing more important than getting to know your grocer. That's not irony. That's real life." When not working the door at the music space/art gallery/puppet theater — the one opened last month by his pals from the free weekly with the "manifesto" to "support local talent"— he is very busy. It may seem as if he spends every day loitering in the neighborhood's last remaining Portuguese café ("There's an authentic culture there, you know?"), but it's more his "makeshift office." The Localist says the retired old men at the café are teaching him chess, but really they steadily ignore him. Which is fine, because The Localist needs to concentrate on the projects he's planning out in his notebook anyway — like the amateur burlesque fund-raising night for Sweetly Cheeseloaf!, the electro-garage-noisecore band that he plays in with his roommate (two-bedroom, flea-market furniture, "crazy" Hasidic landlord) and his roommate's ex-girlfriend (who might be a lesbian now). The Localist is going to give out free passes for the show to all his "buddies" at the café — "Like Puelo! Do you know he used to be a *fishmonger*?" It's just his way of "giving back." Still emails his parents — living a sustained "cultural death" in their faraway, leafy suburb — asking for money when he needs to go to the dentist.

THE PORCH GNOME

AVERAGE AGE: 75
NATURAL HABITAT: Little Italy or Greektown

The Porch Gnome is most often Italian, though he could also be Portuguese or Greek. Found mainly in urban neighborhoods that boast either the word "Little" before the name of a Mediterranean country or "town" after it, The Porch Gnome — a deeply retired type — can be spotted only from April through late September, which is when he takes up his perch on the porch. Significant attributes include the use of indoor furniture, such as upholstered brocade sofas, outdoors. In similar fashion, The Porch Gnome is fond of wearing undershirts as outerwear. May also display copious amounts of classical statuary or religious iconography on his front lawn. Cultivation of tomato plants or grape vines in plastic buckets is common, as is the ability to cram eighteen species of flowers into fifteen square feet of lawn (plaster statues of Adonis and/or the Virgin Mary notwithstanding). Often at war with The Porch Gnome next door, who may or may not have recently installed a working fountain on his own lawn — a peeing cherub, perhaps — thus raising the stakes of one-upmanship to a completely new level. Although rarely seen in winter months, The Porch Gnome has a brief spurt of highly illuminating cold-weather creativity around Christmas.

CRAFTS CATHY

AVERAGE AGE: 23
NATURAL HABITAT: Downtown knitting circle

Crafts Cathy sees herself as part of "a movement of cool girls reclaiming craft." Belongs to a rockabilly knitting group called Rippin' Kittens. Currently thinking of "resuscitating petit point" with a portrait of Elvis ("It will look like a velvet painting, but it will take one hundred thirty-seven hours"). *Hates* Martha Stewart (though the jail angle was "kinda interesting") and is a secret fan of *ReadyMade*, a magazine aimed at "young, hip crafts fans," a subculture that would sound like a punch-line if it didn't actually exist. Crafts Cathy purls with attitude on the subway. She wears knee socks over ripped fishnets and has a black bob over which she may wear a pillbox hat (leopard fun fur pasted onto cardboard). Sews the costumes for a gay retro eighties burlesque troupe called Sassy Slatterns. An inveterate journal keeper (the journal is hand-made; entries are written in a variety of colored pens), she often complains to her diary that she can't find a good guy, although now that she's hanging with the Sassy Slatterns, she thinks she might be a lesbian anyway. For the holidays, Crafts Cathy does not make jam. Last year, for the Rippin' Kittens' Christmas gift swap, she made something called Blood Orange Body Smear, a horror-show take on the fruity exfoliator. This year, her holiday gift list includes: "mid-century modern clock made with plate and chopsticks" (Mom); "disco ball made of Chinese globe lantern with old CDs pasted all over it" (brother); and "voodoo-doll pincushions" (everybody else). Says the dolls reflect Christmas's "true pagan roots."

KRAZY KAL

AVERAGE AGE: 30
NATURAL HABITAT: Logged on to engrish.com

Krazy Kal is a collector. He falls into just one of the subspecies of men in their thirties whose cultural proclivities skew toward the juvenile. Krazy Kal has something he calls his "Great Wall"— essentially, Billy bookcases from Ikea with lots of crap on them. Star Wars figures are too valuable for this breed of stockpiler, who prefers to gather and display gummy candies in rude or disgusting shapes (boobs, snot, garbage cans of worms, etc.); any inexpensive commercial item from Asia, where English words are misused to scatological or absurd effect (packaged foods called Crack Pipe Noodles or Homo Sausage. Or a box of Japanese toilet-seat covers that state: "Take a break, look back at your glory, and feel your natural output"); cheap toys of the vintage joke-store variety (hand-buzzer key rings, invisible-ink pens); and eighties lunch boxes (Transformers, *Pee-wee's Playhouse*). Has never dusted the Billy bookcase. Has not received a birthday present worth more than three dollars in years. Has never dated a woman who found his installation anything more than slightly disquieting.

THE GRAPHIC NOVELIST

AVERAGE AGE: 42
NATURAL HABITAT: Basement studio

The Graphic Novelist despises being called a "graphic novelist"—"a handle invented by snobs too afraid to use the word *comics*." If he seems curmudgeonly, it's because he hasn't left his house in twenty-eight days. The Graphic Novelist is creating his *Epic of Loneliness and Boredom*, part of his *I Am the Saddest Man in the World* series, an ongoing autobiography in which the narrative is composed of nothing but the GN sitting in his basement studio, dreaming about model trains and "sassy dames" in seamed stockings. *The New Yorker* has called the series "riveting—modern Dostoevsky." Lives in a house crammed with ancient comics, newspapers, and obscure cheesecake magazines in a prewar bedroom suburb. Is never seen in public in anything but a three-piece suit and fedora, because "the aesthetic of the world has atrophied since 1935." Carries a very heavy leather satchel wherever he goes, the contents of which remain a mystery even to his long-suffering girlfriend, a calligraphy artist with manic-depressive tendencies. Wears a full-coverage twenties striped bathing costume when he is drawing and writing. It's one of his many quirks that the folks at "those execrable literary magazines that send wide-eyed reporters to my door" find so fascinating. (He also uses baking soda instead of toothpaste and has spent the past three years obsessively reconstructing a *circa* 1910 telephone operator's switchboard in his back shed. When it's done, he has "no idea what its use will be.") The girlfriend tells the GN that if he keeps up his hermitlike existence, he will "die alone, in a cat litter of yellowing paper and telephone wire." At the last Harvey Awards, she fooled around in the bathroom with a "commercial superhero hack" from Marvel while the GN accepted prizes with pretentious haiku speeches, which no one understood.

MONSIEUR JAZZ

AVERAGE AGE: 39
NATURAL HABITAT: Free concert

Takes pride in the fact that he has seen Pat Metheny live at the Montreal International Jazz Festival no fewer than nine times. Has no idea that "jazz fusion" of the Metheny ilk has been the butt of an absurdly large number of jokes in every other corner of the music world for at least twice as many years. Possesses vast amounts of jazz-themed clothing and paraphernalia, such as piano-key scarves, saxophone cuff links, musical-note pins, and many T-shirts bearing cats (or sometimes "kats" or, God help us, "kool kats") playing instruments (pianos, saxophones). When not wearing a fedora, he wears a Utah Jazz cap, even though he's never been to a basketball game (hates sports) or Utah. Also possesses a ponytail around which a single girly elastic can wind seven to eight times. Says "cool" and "man" a lot, often in succession. Has zero musical talent but can play air instruments like nobody's business in mimicry of other "kool kats" at free concerts in the park. Post–jazz fest, tries to hold on to that International Jazz feeling by going to a bar with an indoor brick wall and a vaguely 1989 vibe (while no doubt striving for something more 1949). Has a "smoky" voice that he patented in community college (hosted a radio show called *Night Moves* during his time there). Everyone at his office (the customer-service division of a phone company) thinks he's creepy.

THE DAY TRIPPER

AVERAGE AGE: 48
NATURAL HABITAT: Outdoor cultural festival

Most of us are proud of ourselves if on the odd night we opt for a play instead of a movie. But The Day Tripper is different — a sensible type with an undemanding job, she decided long ago that she would "live like a tourist" in her own city. Every Sunday, she sits down with her weekend newspaper and her local *Time Out* and scans the listings with two different colored highlighters. Knows when any institution is having an open house, when any society needs volunteers, when any musical genre is having a festival, and when any ethnic group is celebrating its food and culture. Is the only person under the age of sixty to ever take the walking tour of pre-Edwardian park statuary that the library offers every summer, and is certainly the only person ever to take both that walk and the one entitled Nature Poetry Al Fresco! in the same day (actually was the only person ever to sign up for Nature Poetry Al Fresco!). Is a friend of all museums and is presently enrolled in a Thai cooking course. Is a member of a choir. Also a member of an online book club. She is one of the two people in the city who can be counted on to attend just about any reading at Barnes & Noble. (The other, nicknamed "Booby" by bookstore staff, is a heavy breather coated in dandruff who fixates on female authors' breasts. The Day Tripper never speaks to him.) At the summer music festivals, she arrives an hour before anyone else, with a fold-out chair. Has trouble with relationships ("too time-consuming") and has few close friends. Most acquaintances who call her do so only when looking for something to do after plans have fallen through with others. Part of the rare female breed that doesn't need a magazine for company when dining alone.

THE YOUNG CLAMB

AVERAGE AGE: Younger than 50
NATURAL HABITAT: "A higher musical plane"

The Young Clamb is the Classical-Music Buff, and, just as an architect need be nothing like young to be considered a "young architect," so with the Clamb. Holds a day job at a library or something suitably archival. Found a couple of times a year at the symphony or at a movie, alone (last film seen: *The Diving Bell and the Butterfly*). Often gay but nothing like those "opera fags" with all their love of pomp and brocade. The Young Clamb is more tweed, sweaters with holes, and corduroy. Drinks tea, not coffee. Has carried the same worn canvas bag, which states "Music Is My Bag," for longer than he can remember. Somewhat bitter after years of being the go-to person for acquaintances looking to find pieces of music they first heard on airline commercials. The owner of four cats (Schoenberg, Schumann, Stravinsky, and Scarlatti) and two Bose Wave stereos (one in the kitchen). Makes weekly trips to the top floor of Virgin, where he has a long-standing crush on the classical section's evening clerk. Will never be seen in the Naxos aisle. Lives in a creaky-floored walk-up with framed Tanglewood posters from the eighties and many ferns in it, plants that, yes, he does talk to. Practices viola on Friday evenings (is a terrible musician) and on Saturday night likes to try new recipes and, sometimes, drink two bottles of Brouilly while listening to Beethoven's *Eroica* (never Beethoven's Fifth) at top volume. Will be spending Christmas with old senile aunt. Has no invitations for New Year's Eve, but "would just as soon spend that most wretched night reading and listening to the new Wiener Philharmoniker."

THE POINTILLIST

AVERAGE AGE: 39
NATURAL HABITAT: Checkout counter

A descendant of the coupon clipper of yesteryear. A close relative to the tax-return obsessive who hoards receipts. Often seen at checkout counters holding no fewer than three pieces of plastic, The Pointillist is a member of at least a dozen reward clubs. Will not buy so much as a newspaper with cash when it could get her points on a credit card. "One newspaper equals two points on my American Express," she says, "so if you think of the loss, paying with cash is like paying twice." Still gnashing over the fact that her teenaged daughter forgot to give the ticket agent her SkyMiles number when flying to see Grandma at Christmas ("And then she threw out her boarding passes — that's one-eighth of a trip to New York down the toilet"). At dinner with friends, she's the first with her credit card out. "Oh, let's make it easy," she'll say. "I'll put it on my card, and you can give me your portion in cash." Has joined three long-distance programs in the past six months because of the points offered on sign-up ("Nothing says you can't cancel the next day"). Increasingly finds herself devoting entire Saturdays to going over statements. Wallet is so bursting with point, reward, and courtesy cards that she now has to wrap a rubber band around it to keep it folded shut ("I don't know who this George from *Seinfeld* is, but a day doesn't go by that someone doesn't mention his wallet when looking at mine"). Realized that perhaps things were getting a bit out of hand when last week she forgot to get a stamp on her Starbucks card after purchasing a $1.50 coffee and walked ten blocks back to the café to get it.

THE BACKGROUNDER

AVERAGE AGE: 35
NATURAL HABITAT: Work desk

You know you are being backgrounded by the ever multitasking Backgrounder when you are talking to her on the phone and all you are getting back is "Uh-huh. Mm-hmm." You hear faint typing. "Are you sending emails?" you ask. "No, no," says The Backgrounder. "I'm listening. Absolutely." Has various ways of "listening," or at least making you think she is listening. There's "Uh-huh. Mm-hmm," for standard chat. There's "Reallllly? Reeaaaally?" when The Backgrounder senses that what she is being told could be categorized as either dramatic or crazy. When an anecdote or rant is finished — and The Backgrounder can always tell, because the person on the other end stops talking and The Backgrounder's typing noises seem to amplify in the silence — she's got two responses. There's the simple "Wow" or the more nuanced "Interesting." The Backgrounder has been working on silent keying and mousing methods, but when she's on Google Talk, she sometimes gets carried away and forgets. When Pam was having "issues" with David last week and needed two hours of venting on the phone, The Backgrounder managed to do all her Internet banking, answer twenty-one emails, and watch an *Arrested Development* episode at the same time. "He's such an asshole," said Pam. Hmm-hmmm. "He has the emotional maturity of a fifteen-year-old." Reeeally? Wow. "No, I swear, he just thinks he can go around and live like a single person, with me waiting in the wings like his mother." Wow. Interesting. "Hey! Are you listening?" "Pam," said The Backgrounder, pressing send on Google Talk and wondering why that bit of downloading was taking so long (and how *Arrested Development* manages to be so funny — the best show in TV? Ever?), "I am totally and one hundred percent here for you."

GREENHOUSE GILDA

AVERAGE AGE: 65+
NATURAL HABITAT: The far side of green

Hannah was no ecowarrior or anything, but something changed in her after watching *Planet Earth* with the kids on the Discovery Channel for ten weeks running. When visiting her mother, Gilda, in Syracuse last week, she had flashes of those helpless polar bears going off in her head. The first trigger was the content of GG's garbage. "Look at this," said Hannah, opening one double-bagged garbage bag in disbelief: ten plastic water bottles, countless newspapers, a phonebook, two extra-large cans of Lavender Breeze aerosol air freshener, and two empty jumbo bags of something called Lawn Magic Weed Killing Fertilizer with Extra-Strength Insecticide. "Mom, this is the kind of stuff creating that nasty algae in the river!" said Hannah. "But we're miles from the river, darling — there's just the canal. And that's *man-made*," replied GG. "Where's your recycling bin?" asked Hannah. "Oh, I use it to keep crafts in," said Gilda. "Now excuse me, I need to check things in the clothes dryer." Hannah thought of the endangered snow leopards and the melting ice cap and that *she must keep her mother away from the dryer*. "I'll do it!" said Hannah, and then, opening the door of the XXL-sized appliance, called out, "There's nothing in here." Gilda said to look closer. Her peds — ladies toe protectors, the smallest garment in existence — were in there. "Mom, do you know how much energy you are using for *peds*?" Hannah needed air. "I'm going to the supermarket to get dinner," she said, picking a plastic bag out from the thousands underneath her mother's sink. "Lovely!" said Gilda. "Pick up some disposable plates and plastic utensils too. We'll save the river by not running the dishwasher tonight. Sound good?"

MR. TICKETS

AVERAGE AGE: 55
NATURAL HABITAT: Shabby office in a nondescript building

No one is quite sure what Mr. Tickets's connections are. He is the guy who gets a call when a mother-in-law's neighbor is in a panic because she promised to take her daughter to Cirque du Soleil as a birthday treat and it is sold out. He's the one who makes it okay when a friend's top client is in town hankering for a big night of basketball and there are no basketball tickets to be had. Worked as in-house counsel at a big TV corporation twenty-five years ago, after which he went solo as a high-flying entertainment lawyer. But then there was that scandal. Now he works from a small, somewhat threadbare office and says he is "in business." He's managed to hold on to some of his minor connections from his big-shot days, but in truth he lost his real connections years ago (about the same time he was disbarred). Still, he can't give up his magnanimous standing as someone who can get anyone tickets at any time, even if these days he sometimes needs to get creative when people call looking for the impossible-to-find. Privately, he felt he'd reached something of a low when he had to resort to calling and then sweet-talking the concierge at the Marriott Marquis last week in order to procure opera tickets for some friend-of-a-friend's friend. Mr. Tickets had told the friend-of-a-friend that he wasn't sure if the opera would be so easy. "Oh," replied the friend-of-a-friend. "Well, my son knows someone who does the listings at that free daily — you know, the one they hand out in the subway? Maybe *he* can help me." It was obvious bait, and Mr. Tickets couldn't help but take it. He figures one day the favors will come back to him.

FELICITY FREEBIE

AVERAGE AGE: 40
NATURAL HABITAT: Launch

Has always said that if you are going to work in PR, then you had better lap up the perks — or, as she calls it, the "schwag"— because "the rest of the biz is people crapping on you." Sundance Film Festival week is the best for free stuff. This Friday alone, Ms. Freebie received a Calvin Klein scarf, a giant chocolate cell phone, a spatula in a massive box of wood chips, and a "reprogrammable crystal." There was also a pair of Motorola boxing gloves, a Rabbit corkscrew care of Village Roadshow, a Focus Features pepper mill, a Showcase carabiner (Ms. Freebie has been the beneficiary of nine carabiners in the past six months and wants to know "just who in the media is needing so much mountain-climbing equipment"), and a hoochy thong, part of J.Lo's new lingerie line. Ms. Freebie's top dresser drawer is full of branded underwear. "Last year, underwear was the new T-shirt in promoland," she says. And while she usually only wears the gratis skivvies on certain days of the month, there was one slip-up after that crazy night at Beatrice Inn where she ended up going home with a guy from PMK/HBH and forgot that her underwear was branded with the name of one of the Big Four accounting firms — using Swarovski crystals, no less — on the backside. It was almost as bad as the fashion week a few years ago when seven battling publicists showed up carrying the same Michael Kors bag that was sent out "exclusively" to every woman in the media. And, speaking of dogs, if anyone is in need of some clothing for their pup, Ms. Freebie is in ownership of about seven "doggy Ts." Apparently doggy Ts are this year's answer to last year's underwear. Felicity misses the good old days when companies just sent booze —"Booze you could regift. I can't go to a dinner party and be like, 'Thanks for having me. Here's a T-shirt for your dog. Don't mind the Bausch & Lomb logo.'"

THE BRAND LOYALIST

AVERAGE AGE: 34
NATURAL HABITAT: Retail outlet

The Brand Loyalist works at an outlet belonging to a massive global retailer — he might be a clerk at your local Blockbuster or the one helping you find a pair of jeans at Gap. The peculiarity of The Brand Loyalist is that he is not bitter about his minimum-wage, mind-numbingly dull job. In fact, he has pledged total allegiance to the company for which he works. Dreams of nothing more than one day making it to head office. May have been called a "joiner" or a "company man" in a different era. Today, is alternately called a "weirdo" or "freaking brainwashed" by his coworkers, who hate their place of work with a passion. The Brand Loyalist is well versed in the lingo of his company. If he works at the aforementioned Gap, he will direct you to "the pullovers on the trestle table." If he works at Starbucks, he will, of course, correct you if you order a medium coffee to go. "A tall Sumatra with legs?" he will ask, as if he has no idea what you are ordering. Enjoys referring to his coworkers as "team" ("Hey, team! Time to buck up for sale season!") and conspicuously wears company paraphernalia, such as a magnetic card for entry into the stockroom or promotional pins, sometimes even during off-hours. Gets a jolt of associative pride when he sees advertising for his company in magazines or on billboards. Extreme BLs might organize pizza parties on their own coin to celebrate "an event" such as the hiring of a new manager or the introduction of a novel product. Believes that the people in head office know who he is and are noting his dedication.

THE REFORMED ADMAN

AVERAGE AGE: 31
NATURAL HABITAT: New York

Went to work as a copywriter for McCann-Erickson straight out of college and was made an instant VP after thinking up a car campaign that "ushered in the SUV era" for moms. His idea was to make the "soccer-and-hockey mom demo" believe that "SUVs are not aspirational but necessary" by convincing them that their children will have no friends if picked up from practice in a minivan. His area of expertise soon became "child coerced adult purchases," relying on the "parent-anxiety quotient" or the "kid-nag quotient" to "seal the family buy." By the time he was twenty-six, he had repackaged beef jerky as a "healthy luncheon snack for tweens" and doubled the sales of one coffee-shop chain by running those notorious "Coffee is cool — it's the BUZZ!" ads featuring a skateboarding dog during Saturday morning cartoon slots. He thought he was burned out so took a cycling trip through Patagonia, where he "had a breakthrough" on a mountaintop and realized that "SUVs are evil and coffee is bad for children." Returned a Buddhist. Was forced to take a sabbatical when he derailed an antacid campaign by refusing to sell the tablets as "a yummy candy for the whole family — with calcium!" Now "nurturing his creativity" through making a self-funded documentary about how "industrial pollution is rendering the entire Atlantic salmon population deaf." Suddenly finds his glass-walled penthouse loft and his D&G–clad girlfriend insufferable. Can't go back to the firm. Contemplating writing a memoir about discovering Gautama.

ALASKA MAN

AVERAGE AGE: 30
NATURAL HABITAT: Up north

Alaska Man read a few books by Jon Krakauer and went up north for the first time when he was twenty-six (and was still a vegetarian). Has returned to Alaska every year since, often on fact-finding missions for the government or to make a documentary film. Is fond of collecting "authentic" experiences when in Tok or Eureka, such as hunting caribou, skinning caribou, and running with the caribou. Says he believes in "knowing the animal you eat." Also says he now feels "out of place when in the southern man's land," forgetting that he himself is the son of two very white accountants from Tampa. When down below the forty-ninth parallel, he can usually be detected by the habit of wearing lumber jackets and T-shirts bearing pictures of dogs pulling sleds, grizzlies fishing salmon, or caribou just being caribou. Might carry a knife in a conspicuous fashion, such as a leather belt holster. Also fond of dropping the term "snowmachine" into everyday conversation ("No one says 'snowmobile' in the real north") and of keeping in his wallet photos of himself on said vehicle, perhaps with a poached baby musk ox tied to its rear. Will arrive at dinner parties with "exotic" dried meat in a Ziploc bag rather than a bottle of wine for his hosts. At the party, will woo the ladies with brave tales of trying to cross the Northwest Passage with nothing but the North Star as a guide. Inevitably bearded.

THE ANTIPOD

AVERAGE AGE: 42
NATURAL HABITAT: Off the grid

The Antipod didn't mean to become a modern-day Luddite, it just happened. He's not a true hater of technology, more just dense when it comes to things digital and communicatory. He's afraid to unplug his VCR setup, so he still has not switched to DVD. He once went to Radio Shack to inquire about cell-phone plans, but it made his head hurt, so he never got one. It was never really an issue until some-time last year, when colleagues began complaining, "We don't know where you are all the time." Which got The Antipod thinking, "Why *should* people know where I am all the time?" So what started as a mild lethargy toward technology turned into a kind of personal badge. Suddenly, The Antipod's use of a pen-and-paper agenda rather than a BlackBerry became a statement. Though not as much as the fact that, on his walks to work, The Antipod could be seen carrying a rather large square object emblazoned with the word *Walkman*. When called on his odd attachment to his cassette player, he answered, haughtily, that his favorite album, by 54-40, was "really hard to find at CD stores." The next day, his colleagues presented him with a half-gift, half-goad: an iPod Nano. When he got home, he plugged it into his IBM (*circa* 1990) and nothing happened. This came as something of a relief to The Antipod, who may even have viewed the hardware's unresponsiveness as a small victory. The present was not a total waste, though. He told his office mates, "Those white earphones make my tapes sound so much better." But then The Antipod said his older headphones are better for keeping his ears warm on cold mornings. "I'll still use those in the winter," he said.

TEEN IN HELL

AVERAGE AGE: 16
NATURAL HABITAT: See title

Jack wanted an iMac. Mom and Dad — who had Jack late — said they would buy him the computer on one condition. "Jack, your mother wants to learn how to use email and the Internet," said Dad. "And I want you to show me how to download music. I need new cardio mixes." The very words *cardio mix* made Jack want to run very far away, someplace where the vision of Dad in shiny shorts could not be conjured up. But Jack just smiled and said, *"No problem — I swear."* Of course, Jack had no intention of helping anyone but himself with the new Mac. All he could think of was endless happy hours of ripping music and watching *Ali G* episodes and naughty webcam fare. It takes Jack just three days to realize that he has done the teenage equivalent of signing a deal with Satan. Now it's all, "Jack, honey, could you remind me how to get into Gmail?" and "Jack, have you downloaded that KC and the Sunshine Band song for my cardio mix yet?" and "Jack, could you please go help your mother? She's punching her email password into the Google search again." Turns out Mom wants to send an email to a spam source. ("Darling, if someone writes you a letter, you write back. Common courtesy. Now, let's begin: 'To whom it may concern: Thank you for your offer of Natural Botox. It sounds very interesting, but . . .'") Yesterday, while punching her email password into Google yet again, Mom stumbled upon Jack's search history, which included requests for "barely legal" and "art-school whores." When confronted, Jack convinced Mom that those terms were planted on the computer "by some crazy virus."

THE LITERARY BLOGGER

AVERAGE AGE: 29

NATURAL HABITAT: Williamsburg basement

A graduate of the creative writing program at Columbia, The Literary Blogger has written a novel, a postironic epic set in "hipster" Brooklyn (quotation marks his), a borough the LB describes as a "shtetl for the soulless." His agent has not been able to sell it, and the LB, who likes the words *my agent* a whole lot and regularly throws in "Yeah, he's Jonathan Safran Foer's agent too," is now "thinking of getting a new agent" (Benjamin Kunkel's). Indeed, even though the LB is a terrible fiction writer, he may, in fact, be able to get Kunkel's agent, because the LB's blog, which is linked to other lit blogs of note, has been on a four-week bashing spree of Kunkel (first posting: "Benjamin Kunkel: The Future of Fiction or Hair Gel Model?"). "He'll take me to shut me up," says the LB. Although he has the persona for bon vivantism, he spends 90 percent of every week in his Williamsburg basement apartment obsessively reading Gawker.com and tending to his own site, which he still insists is "just a hobby." Petrified of turning thirty, the LB fears that if his novel is not published by then, he will have missed the sell-by date of Hot Young Authorism, and he may wind up being remembered as that guy who once got into a fistfight with Jonathan Ames at a PEN party for Jay McInerney.

THE MEMOIRIST

AVERAGE AGE: 22
NATURAL HABITAT: European best-seller list

Currently translated into nineteen languages. Got signed after an agent at Curtis Brown in England somehow received a school notebook in the mail, detailing The Memoirist's lustful (and, ultimately, pornographically consummated) longings for a sociology prof at her university (the class he taught was Football: Game or Metaphor?—a fact obscured in all nineteen languages). Since the publication of *Inverted Commas in Bed*, life's been a whirlwind for The Memoirist, now living in London, dating the Curtis Brown agent, and penning a "kinky yet intellectual" weekly column for the *Guardian*, most recently one in which she advocated bringing back the cane to the educational system ("For me, the milky buttocks have always played a role in education"). Is rumored to be Italian (though she was born in Michigan) due to an overly formal prose style, which sounds translated even in its original English, and her propensity for being photographed wearing leopard print. Writing style actually copped from *Story of O*. Now under pressure to produce a follow-up to her smash debut. On the urging of her agent—who, frankly, can't wait to get the little brat out of his apartment—is considering a "bodice ripper that takes place in a convent." Her agent believes The Memoirist could really find a lot in the "Catholic lesbian angle" and is making preparations to have his beloved shipped to Campania as soon as possible.

THAT YOUNG LITERARY GUY

AVERAGE AGE: 26
NATURAL HABITAT: Book reading

Has just published a novel, half of which is composed of footnotes. The type is so small that most will need a magnifying glass to read it, but Lit Guy says this is not due to his being difficult, it's more "a kind of smallness that I want to convey." His ex-girlfriend, the cartoonist with the really short bangs who did those naive, childlike line drawings of birds for Lit Guy's blog, was overheard at the launch saying that his dependence on kooky form "has the stink of Dave Eggers to it." But, in truth, Lit Guy has nothing of Dave Eggers in him, because he has submitted six short stories and three of his original "backward sonnets" to Eggers's magazine *McSweeney's* and not one of them has gotten in. ("Eggers has lost the plot anyway.") Lit Guy, who only wears suits from the Salvation Army, is "completely pleased" that his own work of genius is being put out by a publisher so obscure no one except the staff at Elliot Bay has heard of it. Not for him the Random Houses and the superagents, all those Slick Ricks hobnobbing at Book Expo, probably with his former roommate from Dartmouth who wrote that piece of trash that is being hailed by the media ("the commercial media") as the next *Life of Pi*. "More power to him," says Lit Guy. "If his final destination is *Oprah*, that's his choice." Has taken to writing his latest work-in-progress — a biography of his mother, a Wyoming housewife ("her ordinariness is the point"), told from the point of view of a fictional lumberjack ("It's Americana. And it's sincere") — with a No. 2 pencil on foolscap ("an exercise in *really considering* words"). Has no problem picking up hot poetesses at readings but is secretly worried that, once they see past his postironic sensitivity, they will find him fantastically boring.

THE NEW DORKER

AVERAGE AGE: 50
NATURAL HABITAT: Newsroom

Both a smug and bitter type, The New Dorker is most often a journalist. He has an obsessive preoccupation with "literary" magazines, such as *The New Yorker*, the *Atlantic*, and *Harper's*. In his twenties, laying type at the local paper, he believed he would one day write for *The New Yorker*, or at least for *Harper's*, but instead he became what he often self-deprecatingly terms a "hack sucking up freebies and pulling stories out of my ass" (a.k.a. a city columnist). Last year, The New Dorker was commissioned to write a four-hundred-word sidebar for a magazine that — perhaps to encourage profitable newsstand confusion — looks an awful lot like the aforementioned titles. But the piece never ran. The editor said it was "too newspapery," as every paragraph in said piece began with a question (e.g., "So what now for sewage treatment?") and was composed of a single sentence (e.g., "So what now for sewage treatment?"). The New Dorker, who believed he had honed a "Gladwellian" style in the piece, assuaged his humiliation by convincing himself that the article was not really nixed by the editor "but by some intern straight out of J-school." He can often be found at his local newsstand, as he has never subscribed to his favorite magazines because a subscription means "getting them one week late." Occasionally gets burnout, where he feels guilty and shackled by a stack of unread issues. Cannot bring himself to throw out his old magazines, a source of contention with his wife, who wants to turn the back room, where he keeps them in stacked milk crates, into a solarium.

MADAME CULTURE

AVERAGE AGE: 60
NATURAL HABITAT: Best seats in the arts amphitheater

After her 1997 alimony settlement, Madame Culture opened an art gallery specializing in ethnic tapestries and "glass art." Asshole ex-husband (investment banker, recently seen about town with that gym-bunny slut of a social columnist) was heard remarking that it's nice that "Cruella finally found something to do with that goddamn degree she wore around her neck for thirty-five years" (art history, Sorbonne, "swinging sixties"). Now Madame Culture — who knows she's more a Paloma than a Cruella — has nothing but chunky Third World costume jewelry, very big belts (at her age! What courage!), and those signature fire-engine red reading glasses weighing down her torso. Known for getting away with other "outrageous" accessories, such as the odd cigarette, a "sharp tongue," and the occasional company of Julio, Venezuelan masseur (and also a poet — the poor boy just needed a patron). Staunch volunteer: opera house, fine-arts museum, ballet. Currently setting up familiarization campaign to "bring the drama and beauty of Seattle's vibrant contemporary dance scene to the world." At a recent event where the dancers performed in the nude, was heard remarking, "Is not the bare skin the true costume of the body?" Considers herself a "decadent." Hasn't had sex in six years.

THE ANCIENT YOUTHY

AVERAGE AGE: 55
NATURAL HABITAT: "Down with the kids"

Not to be confused with the suddenly common mammal known as The Aging Hipster, The Ancient Youthy is a dad- or granddad-aged chronicler of youth who separates himself from the aforementioned hipster type by taking what he calls "only an academic interest" in youth and their culture. Cultural studies and sociology departments are rife with AYs, a type who will go to any length to prove he is not trying to glean dew off the young — being really into Mahler, for instance, and donning unquestionably mature accoutrements such as bow ties, three-piece suits, and, in extreme cases, trilbies (see Tom Wolfe). Unlike The Aging Hipster, The Ancient Youthy will never pepper his conversation with anything resembling a "'Sup?" or a "Suuu-weeet!" unless quoting sources. Will often use air quotes to doubly show these are not "his" words. When he needs to utter terms such as "Gwen Stefani's Harajuku Girls" or "the crunk-a-dunk stylings of Lil Jon," he will pick the line up as if with silver tongs, making his already plummy mid-Atlantic accent even more insufferable — all of which drives those under the age of thirty from the room holding their ears, while those over fifty remain fascinated. "Where does he find this stuff?" they trill. "What a researcher!" Indeed, the AY will sometimes do things like spend an entire month loitering around undergrad cafeterias with a look of placid disdain, but more often he simply watches MTV and reads lots of magazines. At the newsstand, the AY's stack of glossies with titles prefixed by *Teen* has made more than one clerk raise an eyebrow at the possibly insanely perverted geezer buying them. "For your granddaughter?" they ask hopefully. "Their assumption of my barbaric decadence," the AY once said, "is endlessly amusing."

THE OLD GUY AT THE GYM

AVERAGE AGE: ???
NATURAL HABITAT: Weight room

Most members of the gym are sure that they have never been there when The Old Guy at the Gym hasn't been there as well. Perhaps he lives there. He knows all the trainers and regulars by name and obviously takes pride in this intimacy, as he uses their names *a lot*, as in, "I see you are going very hard on the Smith machine, Samantha," or "Hello, Wodjic, how's the knee, my friend, Wodjic?" Nobody has any idea what The Old Guy at the Gym does for a living, or indeed how old the Old Guy is, just that he's the only male in the place who wears miniature Spandex shorts outside of spinning class (with a tank top tucked in), and that his socks always stay miraculously pulled up, even with calves thinned by age. He once referred to a "cow at home," which might mean there is a wife. There is something vaguely European about his long white hair; flattened, antique Superga sneakers; and propensity for hitting himself with a wet towel while naked and dangling in the sauna ("Good for circulation!"). Wodjic, the trainer, says the Old Guy is definitely "not Hungarian or Polish," though, and feels the manner in which the Old Guy yowls a reverberating and somewhat embarrassing "Aaaaaaaaaaaaaaacchhh!" when he's lifting impressive iron is a "sure sign that he is German, because Germans always want you to see how much they are lifting." New females at the gym are given a friendly warning about the Old Guy. "He's very flirtatious, but harmless," Samantha will say. "And if he offers to spot you while you are doing bench presses, just know that he's trying to get your face near his hot pants."

MISS NONINVASIVE

AVERAGE AGE: 34
NATURAL HABITAT: Dermatologist's

Got her first dose of Botox two years ago and was worried it would be the "start of a slippery slope." Has since decided that the odd "shot of a little something" once in a while "is really no different than getting your hair colored. It's almost like putting on makeup, just a bit more permanent." And besides, she is sure she's getting more attention at the office since she got the Restylane to "sensualize" her upper lip. Of course, Miss Noninvasive would never get a face-lift or anything like that, although she doesn't think that there's anything gross about a "possible breast lift when I'm, like, forty, and they start falling. And maybe an eye job too." Felt a bit guilty going to L.A. to do her forehead when her doctor in Connecticut told her that more Botox would be "a mistake of not quite Cher proportions," but the shot she got between her eyes a few months ago created new wrinkles higher up, and she figured once she'd already had some, "nothing wrong with just a little more." The L.A. doctor agreed that "Connecticut is a bit behind in matters of semipermanent beauty" and was also a little concerned about Miss Noninvasive's broken blood vessels around her nose. "There's a darkening around the nostrils," he said. Since then, all she can see is the darkness, and so she is now looking into Intense Pulsed Light Therapy, which "everyone knows is so much better than microdermabrasion." Is two months behind in rent, but feels that the benefit of "looking better than I did when I was twenty-one" outweighs the "light financial strain." Has not raised her eyebrows in a very long time. But she's sure she could if she "really wanted to."

THE SIMPSONS QUOTER

AVERAGE AGE: 35
NATURAL HABITAT: His own private Springfield

In high school, Garrett was the kid who had a *Monty Python* or *Spinal Tap* quote for every occasion. In college, he discovered *The Simpsons* — "in its heyday, when Conan O'Brien was still writing for it" — and his conversation was forever changed. His close friends have always said that his propensity for quoting *The Simpsons* ad nauseam is the reason he can't keep a girlfriend — outlandish if you've never met Garrett but confirmed last week when his latest ex divulged that, even though he's a successful financial trader with "a great sense of humor," he "has a problem." "We were in bed not long ago, and he went 'Hmmm . . . boobies,' like Homer, *except about my breasts*." But the real last straw happened when she stayed over at his place last week and awoke to find him perfecting his Apu accent in the bathroom mirror. "He was in there repeating, 'Tonight I'm going to party like it's on sale for nineteen ninety-nine!' in this Indian voice, for an entire hour." Garrett said he was just preparing his speech for John's fortieth birthday party, and, indeed, that night he delivered an oration with so many Homerisms and kernels of Bart wisdom that nobody had any clue what he was saying. "You've lost it," John told him. "This just in," said Garrett, "go to hell!" "What?" said John. "Sorry," said Garrett, "it's Kent Brockman. Remember that episode? We watched it together, back in undergrad." Garrett feels sorry for those who have just started tuning in to the show in recent years ("too many butt-crack jokes now — and no Phil Hartman!") and sorrier for those who think *The Family Guy* even comes close (although he does secretly watch that too). Spending increasing amounts of time online as quimby_974, notably on dating sites. Has struck up an interesting chat relationship with one simpsonschick999.

KID GRAMPA

AVERAGE AGE: 27 going on 80
NATURAL HABITAT: Favorite booth at the deli

Not to be confused with indie types who wear old-man cardigans ironically or the actually old, Kid Grampa is a young man who has always known that inside him lurks a senior citizen. Had an inordinately close relationship with his zaideh, with whom he used to meet at the deli for matzo ball soup with kreplach and medium-fat smoked meat. Zaideh has passed away now, but his habits, somewhat eerily, have lived on in his grandson. This became particularly clear when KG moved in with a girlfriend and suggested she learn how to cook sweet-and-sour meatballs. Loves talk radio and insists on falling asleep every night listening to call-in shows on a crackly transistor. "I can't sleep with that thing blaring," complained the girlfriend. "My grandmother did somehow," replied KG, forgetting his late grandmother's deafness. Has begun volunteering at an old-people's home, where he reads newspapers to a verbose ninety-seven-year-old ex–labor leader and communist whom he calls "the Professor." Seems increasingly obsessed with the Professor (the girlfriend found a copiously highlighted copy of *The Communist Manifesto* the other day) and has begun frequenting the deli with him. Also has an odd fascination with fifties mambo records and spends hours on eBay searching out titles such as Irving Fields's *Bagels and Bongos*, "a classic from the golden Catskills era." "And speaking of the Catskills," says the girlfriend, "he wants to go there this summer." The girlfriend asked KG if it was not enough for him that she was "the only shiksa from New England who knows how to make sweet-and-sour meatballs?" To which KG only grunted a curt, "Ach! Please! Now shhh!" because *Larry King Live* was starting.

TANNED GRANNY

AVERAGE AGE: 84
NATURAL HABITAT: Condo pool

All the folks at Manor Condominiums know Tanned Granny as "one energetic lady." She is the toast of the Seniors' Follies at the nearby Golden Age Center, where her fan dance, performed in a nude body stocking with sequins "in all the right, or should I say wrong, ha ha" places, is the highlight of the Young at Heart Revue. Her high kick isn't what it was back when her late husband, the famous Minsky, owned the nightclub where Tanned Granny   then milky white and known as "Champagne Suzie"—was a showgirl. But Tanned Granny's motto remains "The show must go on!" She is thus always first in line with one of her tuna egg-noodle casseroles when a poor soul in the building has lost his wife. "Maybe you need a little company? After the shibah, maybe come by for a peppermint schnapps?" After two decades' worth of winters in Boca Raton and summers spent at the condo pool—where Tanned Granny can be found from eight to noon reading Belva Plain paperbacks and smoking Merit 100s even on overcast days—her son the dermatologist says it's a "godly wonder" his mother has not succumbed to "melanoma of the most malignant kind." She tells him he sounds like "an old coot," and even though her skin does resemble that of a deflated basketball, Tanned Granny is sure that with the right lighting she can still give off "some real razzle-dazzle." Her son thinks his mother's preoccupation with sex—or, as she calls it, "the old rum-pa-pa-bump"—is highly bizarre "for a woman of such advanced years." But Tanned Granny just tells him to "put a cork in it." "How did I raise you to become such a square, Mr. Big Shot? A woman's jewel box doesn't fall off at eighty, you know."

SUMMER SPRING

AVERAGE AGE: 24
NATURAL HABITAT: Anywhere awesome for tanning

Summer Spring dates Shorts Guy (the jock one sees in a wintry airport wearing Bermudas, flip-flops, and a straw hat when returning from a warm vacation, knowing full well that hometown elements call for a coat and boots). Similarly, Ms. Spring dresses herself in a mantle of hope. As soon as she has returned from her annual March package vacation, she makes a point of removing all winter clothing from her closet and appears in public with bare legs under gauzy skirts, even when the ground is still covered in snow. She began using bronzing lotions in January and, back from vacation, will maintain her golden hue with weekly trips to a tanning salon. By the time warm weather has truly arrived, she will look like she's been in June forever. Somewhat despised by regular women, who might only realize they have not waxed their legs in several months when the thermometer reaches twenty degrees. Absolutely adored by men, who call Summer's beauty "effortless," when in fact her highlighting (blond—"sandy" at its darkest), skin-upkeep practices, and workout routine eat up extraordinary amounts of time and money. Fond of: nicknames, the word *awesome*, flavored lip gloss, spaghetti straps, anything coconut scented, Mexican beer, and year-round barbecue use. Dislikes: Europe, history, socks, food that requires both a knife and fork, "bad vibes," "people who think too much," and "people who make fun of exfoliation."

THE PREPARED TRAVELER

AVERAGE AGE: 56
NATURAL HABITAT: Next to you on the plane

May hate his job in the civil service, but at least he gets three weeks every year, and those three weeks begin now, which is why he is on an eleven-hour flight wearing a Tilley Endurables hat with mosquito-netting neck guard, a cargo vest worthy of a CNN foreign correspondent, and enough advice about malaria meds with which to regale you for hours. Has had six shots this week at the doctor's and so is feeling a bit "rumbly in the old stomach," but not to worry, for The Prepared Traveler's highly organized pillbox contains what any "seasoned journeyer" might need for "diarrhea," or "diarrhea and constipation mixed," or "nausea," or "nausea from motion sickness," or what The Prepared Traveler simply refers to as "Moroccan Belly." "I hope you've brought some toilet-seat covers," he warns. The Prepared Traveler has several and always keeps "one folded up for emergency" in his money belt. The money belt, of course, is already strapped on, because "you wouldn't believe how much robbery goes on in airplanes when the unsuspecting are asleep." The PT never is asleep on planes. ("Staying up is the best way to conquer jet lag. Would you like to see some digital photos from my last trip?") Should you feign having dozed off, he will squeakily highlight passages in his *Lonely Planet* guidebook, drumming his free hand on his buckwheat travel pillow while whistling songs by Tarkan ("Never heard of him? He's the voice of modern Turkey!") until your eyes open. He is certain you would be thrilled to know more about his Botswanan safari of '99.

THE ALMOST CANADIAN

AVERAGE AGE: 25
NATURAL HABITAT: "United States of Amerikkka"

The Almost Canadian began feeling his "affinity" for "my country's kinder, gentler neighbors" when he left his hometown of Phoenix last year for a month-long trip through Scotland. He was, of course, advised to sew a Canadian flag onto his backpack, "because people will treat you nicer." In the Scottish pubs, people asked him about polar bears. When he returned, he told all his friends that Britain was "too Euro" but that he had fallen in love with Canada. He has never been to Canada, but the statement soon turned into "This country is Bush-whacked — I am moving to Canada. I'm just going to drive to the border and declare myself a political refugee." The AC had visions of attending gay weddings with liberal girls who are hot but kinda go both ways and are into hockey. They'd all leave together and go back to one of the girls' log cabins to listen to Neil Young albums while talking about "books and smart stuff like that." Perhaps they would venture outside to make angels in the white snow, feeling sorry for the sweaty unenlightened the AC left behind in the U.S.A. Watched *CBC Newsworld* last night on satellite, rigid with fear. "It's like TV from the early eighties," he confided to his best friend. "Nothing moving on the screen at all. It's like TV from some communist land." His friend replied that "Canadians are sort of commies, you know. They have to buy their booze in government stores." This gave The Almost Canadian pause. "Man, I'm totally down with the pot-smoking thing," he said. "But going to city hall to get your Bacardi on? That's a bit freaky."

MS. MOVING

AVERAGE AGE: 27
NATURAL HABITAT: Certainly not here

Ms. Moving was overheard at her ten-year high-school reunion saying that she is "actually sort of living here and in New York — it's hard to tell, I go back and forth so much." What she should have said is that once every two months she visits a friend of hers who actually did move to New York, and stays a couple of days for "meetings" and "networking" appointments (actually shopping and energetically circling things in the New York *Times* classifieds in a Broadway coffee shop). Of course, it's "super hard finding a decent Manhattan apartment" but she is "this close to getting a great one-bedroom." A studio won't do, "because I'm not willing to live like a student anymore." Ms. Moving has "done London already." She "lived there for two years" (two months actually — during a backpacking trip in 1997; came back with an accent). She says she is also "thinking very seriously" about Paris, "because if I don't do Paris now, when will I?" Ms. Moving says she "knows Paris well." She has "already lived there too" (two weeks — vacation with the folks, 1994). She loves the way "living there is still really living — you *sit down* to have coffee. You have wine with lunch. It's just more civilized." Of course, Ms. Moving has long known that she's "outgrown" Bismarck, ND. It's "so suffocating here" — "a nonculture." She wants to be where "the action is" and no longer feeling like she is "living in a fake city." If you ask for her email address, she'll give you her Hotmail one because she can "access it anywhere." Has still not moved out of her parents' house because, leaving Bismarck any day now, she just can't sign a one-year lease.

ACADEME ANDY

AVERAGE AGE: 29
NATURAL HABITAT: The academic ladder

Since the publication of his groundbreaking paper "Heideggerian Perspectives on the Fact–Value Distinction in Relation to Post-Versailles Landscape Architecture," in the first issue of the interdisciplinary quarterly *Philosophies >>> Horticulture*, Academe Andy has been fielding offers from academic journals like never before. Four years ago, after an underwhelming stint at the University of Michigan, everything changed at the annual American Philosophical Association Conference, where Andy bedded a notable CUNY prof (an even more notable cougar), who said she was "turned on by his ideas on the *I*" (which, surely, was not completely the case, since Andy stole those ideas right out of Cappelen and Lepore). After the CUNY prof's keynote address ("Contextualism in Epistemology and the Context Sensitivity of *Know*") and several margaritas and "psychedelic blow job" shots at a T.G.I. Friday's type of joint, Andy's fate was sealed. It was only a short hop from the margaritas/blow jobs to a teaching position at CUNY and his current status as the toast of the Heideggerian/horticulturalist scene. "In New York, you have no choice but to find a niche and be cutthroat about it," he says. "It's just the academic culture." Sometimes Andy wonders whether, for instance, grafting proto-existentialism to geometric hedge design is of any use to anyone, but then he'll remind himself that there is always his teaching, which, if he wanted to, he could view as something other than a "necessary evil" that he has to "endure" between publications. (His upcoming paper, "Sartrean Collective Authenticity as Applied to the Dutch Tulip Craze," is bound to be his most important yet.)

THE GOOPHY

AVERAGE AGE: 35
NATURAL HABITAT: At death's door (or possibly just having "a bad allergy day")

The GooPhy is the Google Physician, a nondoctor who has made medicine an extreme hobby. With printed-out pages from the Internet as backup, this type has replaced the classic hypochondriac as the bane of every genuine GP. Despite admonitions to "stop self-diagnosing," a GooPhy enters a doctor's office like a lawyer entering a courtroom, accordion file and all. A regular at wrongdiagnosis.com (the gold-standard GooPhy Web site), a GooPhy usually has an acquaintance in med school with access to Medline, who can be hit up for papers on various illnesses and their treatments. Evenings that begin with a simple check for email or movie listings on the Internet can often devolve into an eight-hour odyssey into the vortex of online medical resources. An enlarged vein on a GooPhy's temple becomes — without question — the sign of a tumor ("When you find a bump on one side but not on the other side, you *have* to worry"), and a reaction to cat dander might be interpreted as shingles, a case of scabies, or — you never know — a sign of flesh-eating bacteria. Other typical GooPhy behavior includes compulsively using Purell hand sanitizer, using paper towels to close faucet knobs in public restrooms, and having a veritable pharmacopoeia of supplements in the fridge (Greens+, Omega-3, etc.) and an outsized fascination with the character played by Hugh Laurie on *House*. A GooPhy may take notes during commercials that end with "Ask your doctor about Fortura!" and then actually ask her doctor about Fortura.

THE NOUVEAU HYPO

AVERAGE AGE: 32
NATURAL HABITAT: Homeopathy aisle

Was feeling "blah." A creeping fatigue. Has left the "Philistine" "conventional" doctor who for years told her she was a hypochondriac and should "take a nice vacation." Her homeopath, after all, has decided that her pH levels are surely "unbalanced." Toxins "running rampant." Has now cut out all dairy, wheat, fruit, sugar, caffeine, alcohol, vinegar and other fermented products, and anything packaged or processed. Also no chewing gum ("a tease to the stomach"), no regular toothpaste ("saccharin-filled"), no herbal tea ("nothing more than a mold delivery system"), no tofu ("fermented!"). Is *definitely* feeling more energetic on a diet of organic meat, raw pecans, and leafy greens, although she forgot to take Yakult and garlic supplements today, which may account for the tinge of what The Nouveau Hypo is sure must be the beginnings of Irritable Bowel Syndrome. Or maybe the candida has returned? She does feel a bit yeasty. Also, her lower back still feels "tingly"— that tingle that comes before pain, you know?— but an osteopath recommended by her homeopath assures her that as soon as the five-hundred-dollar custom-made orthotics are ready, this will be righted. At a friend's wedding this past weekend, everyone assumed The Nouveau Hypo — who ate only salad ("oil, no vinegar, please") and the filet ("and it was packed with hormones, for sure") — was on Atkins. "I'm not on a *diet*," she proclaimed, mortified, to her toxin-filled tablemates. "I'm on a *wellness* regimen!" Cried a bit in the bathroom while everyone else tucked into crème brûlée. Mood swings. She'd better call her homeopath.

THE WATER CONNOISSEUR

AVERAGE AGE: 40
NATURAL HABITAT: High-end shopping district

The Water Connoisseur (Fiji still, Badoit sparkling) is not just a connoisseur of water but also of toothpaste (Marvis), notebooks (Muji), paper (Smythson), apples (organic Jonagold "Limited Edition"), office chairs (Aeron), deodorant (Byly), salt (Fleur de Sel de Camargue), chapstick (Kiehl's Lip Balm #1), pajamas (Ralph Lauren), earphones (Bang & Olufsen), steak (dry-aged Angus), tea (silver needle white), and scented candles (Diptyque; "L'Artisan Parfumeur is such a *fraud*"). He's $76,000 in debt but unable to bring himself to buy a lesser toilet paper than Cotonelle, or a more economical breath mint than Altoids. He says there is no point, as the inferior product would go unused (so accustomed is this ass to small luxuries). If he were living in an earlier era, The Water Connoisseur might have been an expert in antiquities or art or maybe, rarely, gastronomy, and not things used to scent armpits or hydrate lips. Spends much time organizing items in his home, even the things in his fridge, in case anyone should stop by. May have some close and needling proximity to wealth, such as a rich ex-wife or a parent who remarried into wealth. Says he "prefers taxis to driving" and "likes the freedom of renting" to explain his lack of car and house, when the truth is he could never afford the sort of vehicle or home that would be in sync with the smaller accessories he spends his money on. He often suffers under a cloud of depression after returning home from shopping, once his purchases have been taken out of their boxes and tissue paper, revealing themselves, ever so briefly, as overpriced toothpaste and notepaper.

THE BAGUETTE

AVERAGE AGE: 32
NATURAL HABITAT: Accessories department

The first one was bought on a whim. She had landed a consulting contract that was short on work but, miraculously, very well paying — "like winning a lottery" — so she decided to get herself something "completely decadent." "It will be like I never *had* the money" was the rationale. The slouchy Bottega Veneta bag, in woven white leather, cost $3,000. Ridiculous, she knew, but she had "never bought anything like that before, so okay." Until that purchase, she had always carried a canvas messenger bag, but soon she needed something for an evening event, and her old clutches seemed shabby next to the Bottega she carried to the office. The Gucci with the jeweled charm was "the fanciest thing" she'd ever bought, and its "extreme uselessness" ("I can't even fit my wallet into it!") made her feel like she was "investing in art" rather than a bit of fabric and ornament at a cost equal to 1.5 months' rent ($2,000). The white Bottega soon turned dingy, and no amount of protector spray could save it. She bought a tan Fendi Spy ($2,500) and then a Balenciaga Motorcycle bag on eBay (a steal at $500!). Then she got a Chloé Paddington (don't ask) and a Mulberry (vowed to make lunches at home for the next eight months). Now she's given to spouting a "theory" on the "mania" that has women sighing with relief when a desired bag is "only" $1,000. Said theory is derived from articles in fashion magazines written by other women who can't stop purchasing expensive handbags and invariably includes something about the bag as womb or the bag as empowerment. Has no idea where next month's rent is going to come from. Would sell the Fendi on eBay if 318 others weren't now trying to do the same thing.

THE EUROPRENEUR

AVERAGE AGE: 40
NATURAL HABITAT: First-class lounge

A bachelor still in possession of the peculiarly British ability to "go mental" until six in the morning and wake up at eight in fully functional work mode. Just back from Kate Moss and Jade Jagger's big party in Mustique and now Heathrow-bound again to close that big contract with T-Mobile. Says he's a "throwback to 2000, and that's just the way I like it, mate!" Not many can afford to be a "staunch flexecutive" anymore the way the Europreneur can, cutting a disheveled-cool figure in his Muji jeans and custom Adidas sneakers, flipping his cell phone and pushing back his copious bangs in first-class lounges across the European Union. And though he would have shuddered to be called a sellout ten years ago, back when he launched that "street-culture style bible" on which he's built his present consultancy (Confusion Ltd., named, of course, after the New Order track of the same title), today he finds those "'keeping it real' issues so incredibly 1991." Was worried that he would never recover from what he has dubbed his "Great Pot Noodles Cock-Up" of 2002, when he told the makers of said instant noodles that "DayGlo Japanese cyber" was the way to go for their youth-oriented campaign (it should have been "postironic American garage revival"; he sees that now). Has found himself dreaming lately of retiring to a villa in Spain. The sun might bleach out that increasingly nagging feeling that at forty he has no business selling himself as the "voice of youth" anymore (he secretly thinks "all hip hop sounds the same"—a bad sign). Not that his clients have any idea.

MOTHER OF REINVENTION

AVERAGE AGE: 44
NATURAL HABITAT: The spotlight, well airbrushed

A celebrity type, the Mother of Reinvention is a woman who enjoyed fame in the eighties, or even the nineties, and has now returned to reap more rewards. While an MOR may have certain cougar attributes, her main target will always be her younger self—a younger man as arm candy is just part of the package. Some MORs never quite go away, they just keep on morphing (Madonna); some go into hibernation after several bad career moves and then redebut (Demi Moore, Carmen Electra); and some achieve truly notable fame only "late in life," thanks to their ability to be over forty and look "hotter than ever" in a white bathing suit (Teri Hatcher). A subset of the MOR is the aged supermodel who returns to the catwalk "sharper and wiser" and often brandishing a cause (Christy Turlington's yogic-emphysema rebranding is the benchmark). While decreased facial mobility due to Botox and filler injections is a signature trait of the MOR, so are statements such as "I don't believe in that kind of stuff. Who would inject poison into her head?" The public, obviously, is meant to suspend disbelief, as no MOR worthy of column inches is ever far from "photos from the vault"—pictures taken a decade or so ago when she was less slim, less toned, and had less lip volume. The idea is that the star has "lost her baby fat" and has aged "gracefully." Successful MORs will often give an ironic nod to their own past or persona—witness Madonna's 2005 club-land-aerobics look, Cindy Crawford's posing in eighties Spandex, or Pamela Anderson, period.

EVERY DAUGHTER'S WORST NIGHTMARE

AVERAGE AGE: 45
NATURAL HABITAT: Hip hop dance class

Chloe's mother was the "coolest chick" in college, which is fine by Chloe, but, as she repeatedly points out to her mother, college is O-V-E-R. "Mom," says Chloe, "you are, like, almost fifty. Act your age." Chloe's mom is obsessed with watching *The O.C.* and *Gossip Girl.* She also has a propensity for stealing Chloe's 7 stretch jeans and then asking her daughter whether "Mommy still looks hot." "Mom," Chloe will reply, "nobody says 'hot' except Paris Hilton." But Chloe's mom "kinda digs" Hilton, and has even been asking her personal trainer to change her program from concentrating on "Madonna arms" to going for something more "Hilton lean," in preparation for Chloe's Sweet Sixteen. Chloe doesn't want the party, but there has been no stopping her mother, who has decided on a "Hip Hop Bling" theme for the event. "Should we put condoms in the bathroom of the party hall?" Mom asked Chloe, to which Chloe replied, "I'm going to do my homework," because she knew it was her mother trying to have another mother-daughter-as-BFFs "convo" about sex. Chloe called Samantha. Samantha said she thought Chloe's mom is amazing. "What? Hold on, Samantha, I can't hear you. MOM! Would you *please*?" Chloe's mom was playing Jay-Z again. "Samantha, in a minute she's going to tell me to come 'bounce' with her," said Chloe. "It's her new thing since she's been taking that retarded hip hop dance class." At which point Chloe's mom yelled from downstairs, "Chloe! Come *bounce with me.* WHOO!"

THE CODDLED DOG

AVERAGE AGE: 4 (28 in dog years)
NATURAL HABITAT: Hermès dog cushion

Caroline had a baby and gave Pinky to her sister Tabitha. "I thought it would be good for her to have something to take care of," said Caroline. Pinky, quite frankly, does not even know how he survived before the changeover. Caroline used to take him to that filthy dog run and feed him Iams. With Tabitha, who is forty and childless, he gets lean steak and salmon filet cut into tiny pieces and mixed with organic flaxseed and olive oil. Pinky's water bowl is attached to a spring water dispenser that is kept fresh by the same H_2O At Home guy who services Tabitha's cooler. Tabitha brushes Pinky's teeth twice a day with chicken-flavored toothpaste. She says that Pinky was "abused" by Caroline, because Caroline let Pinky walk "bare pawed" on salty winter sidewalks. "*We* don't walk barefoot on salty sidewalks. Why in the world should a terrier?" The booties are Vuitton, a purchase that was a bit of a laugh, but then, once Pinky had the footwear, "it was hard not to go the whole way." Now Pinky has collared Polo T-shirts and a Versace lambskin jacket, which sometimes Pinky confuses for prey and tries to eat. His collar and leash are Burberry plaid. Tabitha barely travels anymore — Pinky needs her, and the last time she went to St. Barts and left him at the Pampered Pup Hotel and Spa, she came back to find Pinky "completely depressed and terrorized by an obnoxious toy greyhound with a Napoleonic complex." Caroline told Tabitha that the dog could stay with her in the future, but Tabitha will never take her up on the offer. She knows Caroline would give Pinky tap water, "and the last thing I need is a dog with lead poisoning."

THE EXPECTANT MOTHER (Freaking-Out Edition)

AVERAGE AGE: 33
NATURAL HABITAT: Prenatal class

It's the last trimester, and Kim has just bought *What to Expect When You're Expecting*, a guide to pregnancy that Kevin says has turned her into a lunatic. Kim agrees that the book has caused some anxiety. "Still," she says, "Kevin just doesn't understand." Being a man, Kevin agrees that it's difficult to understand how it would feel to be a pregnant woman. This impediment notwithstanding, he thinks Kim has gone "a bit extreme" in that she no longer lets him wear antiperspirant ("The metal in it can seep out of your armpit," she says, "and into our baby's brain!") and has banished all dairy products from the house ("Fetal lactose intolerance is so common, Kevin"). Kim went into a rage last night when Kevin made dinner and dinner was salmon ("Kevin, do you know how toxic salmon is? It's almost as if you want a damaged baby!"). When he drank a glass of wine, she claimed he was trying to taunt her. He replied that the sky wouldn't fall if Kim had one glass. "In fact, in France, they encourage you to drink wine when you are pregnant — and eat cheese. Lactose-laden!" Kim said she's certain France has "fewer geniuses and many more leaky guts per capita because of that kind of selfishness." She has been reading poetry to her stomach lately, but after yesterday's salmon debacle, she just didn't have the energy for Frost. She was pensive. "People have been doing this for millennia," she told herself. "It shouldn't be so hard. It's the most natural thing in the world." For the next five minutes, she was calm. Then she asked Kevin to bring her some tea tree oil. "Two tablespoons orally every day," she reminded him, "or our baby will have problems with infections."

ADULT G

AVERAGE AGE: 32
NATURAL HABITAT: Just over the hill

Adult G does not totally realize that he falls into the aging hip hop category, because his high era of rap fandom was the late eighties to nineties (A Tribe Called Quest, Public Enemy, then Wu-Tang) and not, for instance, the Whodini era, when rappers wore tight vinyl pants. Still young enough to take ironic pleasure in throwing out the odd "cold lampin'," but not young enough to realize that no one under thirty (who know Flavor Flav only as "that ugly little guy on *The Surreal Life*") will even vaguely understand what he means. Truly believes that no hip hop today is as good as hip hop was when he was eighteen. Is unaware that he thinks this because he is old rather than for reasons that have anything to do with the quality of the music. Lost his interest in contemporary rap around the turn of the millennium, with the upswing of "bling bling" and then Eminem. Got a bit excited about OutKast but has trouble maintaining that interest and can often be found in his car blaring Dr. Dre's *The Chronic* (1992). In fact, was playing that album yesterday while driving with his son, Christopher, age four. Suddenly found the lyrics "very extreme" when Christopher asked, "Daddy, is Mommy a biatch?" Today, played the Buena Vista Social Club while taking Christopher to soccer. Adult G stopped wearing a baseball cap and long basketball shorts last year, when Christopher said, "Daddy, does Mommy dress you too?" Had a sinking feeling when he found a copy of *Vibe* magazine and read it with interest before realizing the issue was from 1995 and didn't even look dated to him.

THE WANNABE FATHER

AVERAGE AGE: 37
NATURAL HABITAT: In limbo

Would stop short of saying his "biological clock is ticking." But actually, he can feel the hands of time cutting away at his "increasingly fragile, or at least it feels that way," sperm count. At thirty-seven, he is divorced, but he's assured by friends that his first hitch-up, which bore no spawn, was just a "starter marriage." Has a steady job at the university, has paid off his mortgage, and has a girlfriend of four years who "one day, God willing," will agree to marry the WF. She — a minor TV personality — is just waiting for what she calls the "right time" in her career, "because to me marriage means babies, and babies mean my life changes in a way that yours doesn't, honey." He says he does not want to be a first-time dad at forty. She reminds him that she is a "full seven years younger" than he and that none of her "girlfriends are thinking kids yet, honey — your friends are just an older, more suburban type," and, besides, "Saul Bellow had a child in his eighties, and I am sure he was a wonderful and capable father to that child." Still, the WF has found himself doing strange things lately: smiling into strollers at the supermarket, insisting on babysitting for colleagues at the expense of media openings with his better half, and pausing his channel surfing at Huggies commercials. Has also taken to perusing baby-name Web sites. His girlfriend has noticed and has asked him why he "can't look at porn instead, like normal men." She says if he could "only hold on one more year," then she "may be ready to think about it." He reminds her that that's what she said last year.

BABY EINSTEIN

AVERAGE AGE: 6 months
NATURAL HABITAT: Playpen

Baby Einstein remembers the good old days, back in the womb, floating weightlessly as Mother played those interesting avant-garde compositions into her stomach using her BabyPlus Prenatal Education System. If Baby Einstein could talk, he would tell Mother that he found BabyPlus's tonal pieces, which the company touts as "scientifically designed audio lessons derived from the familiar 'language' of the maternal heartbeat," far superior to the mundane classical schlock she's taken to playing him now, music thought to be "good for developing babies." "If I hear Vivaldi's *Four Seasons* one more time," thinks Baby Einstein, who considers baroque overrated, "I might very well be quite ill." Of course, Mother, a little dim-witted, does not understand his protestations of kicking and waving. "She says I'm dancing," says Baby Einstein. Reared from birth in the school of educational DVDs, Baby Einstein, if he could speak, would tell his mother that he has quite outgrown his present library of Baby Newton, Baby Bach, and Baby Jackson Pollock ("Pollock! An infant half my age could create those canvases!"). As for those "numeracy" toys, Baby Einstein much prefers the total encompassment of physics to the single-dimensionality of math. Of course, Mother has no idea. "Oh, look how cute," she will say, "he's smiling at the TV! Our smart little boy!" "Note to self," thinks Baby Einstein, "once the gift of word formation descends, alert Mother to the fact that the corners of a mouth turning up can often signal a wincing discontent rather than pleasure. Now where are my banana slices? I feel lacking in potassium."

CAMP KID

AVERAGE AGE: 11
NATURAL HABITAT: The "wilds"

All the cool kids were going to Camp Thousand Pines, and so Camp Kid really, really wanted to go too. That Camp Thousand Pines is populated by the spawn of parents several times richer than Camp Kid's are was not among Camp Kid's considerations. "Mom, *everyone* is going. And then they will all be friends and I will be a *loser*." Camp Kid spent seven miserable days at Camp Thousand Pines before deciding that he really, really wanted to come home. All the other kids descended with duvets and boom boxes and cases full of Pop-Tarts and Kraft macaroni and cheese and massive bags of gummy bears from Costco. But Camp Kid's mom only bought what was on the camp list, and so he arrived with nothing of the sort. When Jonathan J.'s bag of sour snakes went missing, he accused Camp Kid of "stealing" because he's "poor." Then Jonathan S. accused Camp Kid of tattling on him and Jonathan R. for smoking behind the mess hall. Faked sick three times — once by giving himself hickies along his inner arm and then claiming he was "poisoned by ivy" — until the nurse advised the camp director that maybe Camp Kid was having "adjustment problems." The director allowed Camp Kid one phone call home. "Mom, please. *Please*. I'll do anything. Come get me." Camp Kid was crying so hard that Mom started crying too. Then Dad got on the phone. "Son, visiting day is a week away. We'll come up and we can discuss the situation." When visiting day came around, Mom and Dad took Camp Kid to Golden Griddle, and Camp Kid said that everything got better after a counselor found a bag of sour snakes under Random Zack's bed. Now he says he wants to come back next year for the full two months. To which Dad dryly replied, "Second mortgage," to which Camp Kid replied, "What?"

EVERY MOTHER'S WORST NIGHTMARE

AVERAGE AGE: 14

NATURAL HABITAT: Bedroom (door locked)

Describes herself as "fourteen going on fabulous" and has decided that everyone has to call her Elle instead of her real name. (Leslie. Like, *how lame?*) Is totally positive that Mom has been listening in on her phone calls. (Like, last week? When she was on the phone with Lindsay? And they were talking about threesomes? She heard some weird whimpering noises and then a click. *Totally* Mom listening.) From now on it's going to be *only* cell phone, and Mom won't be able to freak about the bill because it'll totally be Mom's *own fault* for *eavesdropping*. Mom's been particularly nosy since finding that cute thong Elle bought at Urban Outfitters ("So what if it says 'Pussy' on the front, Mom? There's a *picture of a cat* under the word") and since Elle started wearing the necklace her new boyfriend (eighteen, and the best poker player in school) gave her. Mom was like, "Is that a roach clip around your neck?" and Elle was like, "Jigga, pleeease!" and Mom was like, "Don't call me Jigga, you're not from the ghetto, and *stop rolling your eyes like that*," and Elle was like, "What*ever*!" Then Mr. Poker text messaged Elle —YR HOTR THAN PARIS, meaning Hilton — and invited her to prom. Now Elle has been coming home late from school with her skin an increasingly deep shade of tan. Mom asked if she was going to the tanning salon. Elle answered, "Yo, I *need* to." Grandma gave her money to buy a dress for prom, and Elle found one, but she needs to be "tanned everywhere" to wear it because the dress "shows major ass cleavage." Mom — who will need to have a word with Grandma — said she hopes Elle "wears a shawl." (Mom has no idea that pashminas are sooo 2000.)

THE GENIUS RETARDE

AVERAGE AGE: "Wise" beyond his years
NATURAL HABITAT: State of confusion

The opposite of the idiot savant, The Genius Retarde is the youngest ever American to receive a Rhodes Scholarship. Currently consulting for NASA from Oxford and writing his doctoral thesis, "which models the paleohydrology of a lake at the summit of Mauna Kea as an early Mars analog." Could not come home for Thanksgiving because he lost his passport. "So get a new one," said his mother. "Where?" asked the GR. "I don't know, go to the American embassy or something." The GR spent hours trying to find the American embassy in London. He finally went into the Mexican embassy, because he figured they would know where the American one was. By the time he got to the U.S. embassy it was closed, which is when the GR realized that he had lost his wallet. Upon returning to Oxford (he hid in the train's WC when the conductor came around), the GR also found his keys were missing. He was forty minutes late for dinner with his thesis adviser, Dr. McInnis. Dr. McInnis told him that all this "forgetfulness seems caused by a heart long unattended to" and set up the GR with his niece. On the date, the niece asked the GR what his favorite movie was. He said *Top Gun*, because *Top Gun* was the only movie he could think of on the spot. He then asked her — really loudly, for some reason — if she found "Tom Cruise sexy, because I find him very sexy!" He said it to make her feel like it was "okay to think Tom Cruise is sexy," but the GR knew the words were wrong and almost saw them tumbling from his mouth in slow motion. She asked if he was gay. He replied, "No, just very cheerful! HAHAHAHA!" He went home early. He couldn't find his house keys again, but luckily the front window was open.

NOT-GAY GAYLORD

AVERAGE AGE: 37
NATURAL HABITAT: In the closet? Not? Who knows?

Not-gay Gaylord isn't a "metrosexual"—all his friends agree that's the wrong description. Gaylord wouldn't be caught dead in a spa and wouldn't know what to do with moisturizer or lululemon yoga capris. Still, everyone thinks he is gay—"except those who think I am Jewish"—especially his gay friends (he has a lot of gay friends). Gaylord even tried being gay once, to see if everyone was right, but he says he could not "go through with it." Has an endless string of girl-friends and a string of breakups just as long. Linda got the boot "because she slurped her soup—I just couldn't stand it." Jordana "had this twangy cadence to her voice," which drove Gaylord "up the wall." Sylvia—gorgeous, artistic, and extremely well mannered—was beyond reproach. Gaylord says he would have moved in with her if she hadn't left him. "She says I channel the spirit of a twelve-year-old girl," said Gaylord, "because I spend four hours on the phone every night chatting with friends." There was also the incident when she caught him ironing his underwear. Gaylord and Sylvia still go to the bakery together every Sunday to buy bagels, a little ritual. The woman at the bakery's cash register once told Gaylord she had a "nice daughter for a nice Jewish boy like you." "I'm not Jewish," Gaylord told her. "Oh, I see!" she said. "You are not going with women! Of course!" Sylvia is too polite to divulge that in bed, Gaylord is not the most conventional hetero male. Linda, however, did let it slip that Gaylord "prefers what he calls 'cuddling' to nearly anything else." Friends have lately put him down as being "asexual." "I think he puts all his sexual energy into keeping his house neat," says Sylvia. "One day, I'm sure that will make some woman very happy."

THE GAY-WEDDING PLANNER

AVERAGE AGE: 60
NATURAL HABITAT: Gay-pride parade

It was about a year ago that event planner Lillian Silberstein realized that "that little shit" from Ultimate Entertainment had her beat. The "little shit" used to work for Lillian, but if an article in *American Jewish Life* was anything to go by, now he was "redefining the bar mitzvah circuit" with an "urban edge and party themes like 'old skool flava.'" "I don't know from flava," she told her assistant. "A chocolate fountain? *This* I understand!" Lillian's assistant told her she "needed to break out of bar mitzvahs and find a new niche." As luck would have it, Paul and Jeffrey came to see Lillian that very week. They wanted a "magnificent wedding, with no gay clichés, like no 'Y.M.C.A.' dance at midnight." "But everyone loves 'Y.M.C.A.' at a wedding," said Lillian. "Too gay," said the couple. "The Village People are gay?" said Lillian, who admittedly has come a long way since then. Now she's the only party planner in the city who offers the option of rainbow-striped chuppah and a dessert table centered by a four-foot ice Adonis with champagne spouting "from his woo-woo." She's in tight with the LGBT-friendly reverends, who Lillian says "aren't Jewish or Catholic or Protestant but *nothing*." ("Lillian, interdenominational is more like *everything*," corrects the assistant.) Lillian had a booth at the last gay-pride parade, but the assistant was sick, so she recruited her husband, Mort, to hand out flyers. "Look lively, Mort!" she yelled from behind the booth. "Try to fit in!" "But I'm not gay!" said Mort, who is sixty-two and a notary. "Morton, we're here, we're queer, get used to it," said Lillian. "Who's *we*?" asked Mort. "The gays!" "You're gay suddenly?" "Mort, just give out the flyers and then we'll go for Chinese."

THE HALLOWEENIUS

AVERAGE AGE: 28
NATURAL HABITAT: Costume party

The Halloweenius is the Halloween genius. He wows the crowds every October 31 with his costume. Will always say he "just slapped it together" but in truth spends months on his ensembles, which are the kind that disallow sitting or anything having to do with toilets. Was obsessed with prosthetic makeup and Sam Raimi movies in high school and now works in the special-effects department of a film company. Thinks of October 31 as his "limelight night." Looks down on those who believe Halloween is for kids, and the women who think it "nothing more than a good excuse to dress like hookers." Two years ago, he won first place at three different costume contests with his Guggenheim Bilbao, a re-creation of the entire building made with pourable foam and attached to The Halloweenius's shoulders using a rejigged ski rack. Last year's "paparazzi" getup — a conglomeration of latex heads, stuffed gloves, and thirty cameras and flashes that really flashed — was so heavy that it caused him serious back pain. At his best friend's blowout party, he smiled through the ache only to get second place in the costume contest, losing out to "Blue Balls," which was that idiot Dan with a bunch of spray-painted tennis balls velcroed onto a sweatshirt. Unthinkingly, he directed his outrage at Julie, Dan's slightly fragile girlfriend, who already felt insecure because she had the worst costume of the night — red one-piece long johns with "Heinz Catsup" scrawled in black marker on the front. "And who the bleep says catsup anyway? It's *ketchup*," ranted The Halloweenius, tearing though the crowd, his costume flashing and his bladder bursting. He apologized to Julie the next day ("Hey, Jules, dressing up like a condiment is totally cool!"). This year, he says, he is "going more streamlined."

THE OFFICE PARTY PLANNER

AVERAGE AGE: Comes alive but once a year
NATURAL HABITAT: Office party

Last year, Janet's Secret Santa gave her a T-shirt that said "Da OPP"—a reference to her status as the firm's perennial Christmastime office party planner. This year, she began emailing memos entitled "HOLIDAY HAPPENINGS" in September, divided into categories such as "Decorations Committee Meeting Minutes." The OPP has always loved Christmas and secretly told Amy, the receptionist, that she misses the old days "when you could just call a Christmas party a Christmas party," although she understands that "a person must be sensitive to the honor of the Jews and of the Muslim community." Amy pointed out that there are no Jews and no Muslims in the office. "What about Lee?" asked the OPP. "Oh, she's a Buddhist or a Zen or something," answered Amy. The OPP sent out an "EMERGENCY PARTY MEETING" email. The meeting was convened at Wendy's. Only Amy came. Over taco salads, the OPP told Amy she was ordering banners from Kinko's that read "Happy Hanukkah" ("or Chanukah?") and "Have a Kwazy Kwanza" ("Qwanza?") but was stumped "about what to do for our Asian coworker." Amy and the OPP decided to get "that guy who plays that Chinese string instrument in the subway" to provide some "Oriental" musical entertainment. On the night, Lee — a third-generation Japanese American — asked the OPP why she had opted for a sitar player instead of a DJ. Nobody was dancing. Finally, Eric, who had arrived wearing a sprig of mistletoe attached to his belt buckle and an "I Love the Ho Ho Hos" T-shirt, sourced a portable stereo. By the time of the Secret Santa exchange, they had listened to *Big Shiny Tunes Volume 9* four times. Eric, the OPP's Secret Santa, bought her penis-shaped pasta from the novelty condom store. Mortified, she made fast friends with the punch bowl. Last seen crazy-dancing with the sitar player to the seventh playing of OutKast's "Hey Ya!"

THE NEW YEAR'S EVE BOYCOTTER

AVERAGE AGE: 29
NATURAL HABITAT: Home

The New Year's Eve Boycotter can actually be any age, as long as it's younger than the age at which people truly do prefer to stay in. While all prospective NYEBs think theirs is the most brilliant idea ever descended from party heaven ("I'm just not going to go out!"), it's a rare NYEB who willingly dons the mantle for more than one year, as they usually find that it's a sure recipe for depression. The NYEB is invariably someone who had an RBNYE (Really Bad New Year's Experience) the previous year. This can involve fondling people one would never normally fondle, mixing incompatible alcoholic drinks, or having to walk home in icy slush at five in the morning with one shoe missing and arriving at the front door only to discover one's keys are missing. "Not this year!" thinks the NYEB. He will have high hopes for his evening in and may carry a whiff of pretension about it too. ("Who *needs* to be out when every idiot in the city is out?") Knows "watching the ball drop" is no fun, so plans to "ignore the fact that it's the thirty-first" by watching DVDs all night (marathons of the show *24* seem a popular choice). The plan works until about 11:59 p.m., when, of course, the NYEB flips the channel to watch the ball drop, feels the depths of his loneliness, and goes to sleep with the squealing sounds of nubile girls looking for action on the street just outside his window. Wakes up at eight in the morning on New Year's Day and feels the intense need to call someone. Has to settle for the only person who might be up (usually a parent) and then finds himself berated "for calling so early on the one morning everyone sleeps in."

THE NAME-DROPPER

AVERAGE AGE: 55
NATURAL HABITAT: Interminable dinner party

Recently did "a spot of Holocaust memorial fund-raising for Steven, who is just so busy with his latest film." When someone asks her to pass the gravy, she just can't do it without giggling because she remembers this "hysterical story" about her "very close friend Teresa involving spilled 57 Sauce." Would claim discretion if she were ever asked why she only uses first names. In truth, she wants you to believe that she is so tight with the likes of Spielberg and Heinz Kerry that surnames are just not necessary. Loves sending out mass emails to "spread awareness" about "good causes." Often "accidentally forgets" to use the blind cc feature. You got her recent one about children in Darfur, and so did philiproth@yahoo.com, bezos@amazonbooks.com, and dionceline@videotron.ca. Philiproth@yahoo.com has already asked The Name-Dropper nine times to "kindly remove me from your list. I do not know who you are." His last email contained an all-caps "PLEASE!" In a minute or two, she will no doubt find a way to reveal that she's "been emailing nonstop with her friend Philip. Authors write the most expressive emails, don't you think?"

THE PEEB

AVERAGE AGE: With that beard, no one is quite sure
NATURAL HABITAT: PBS

The Peeb has worked at PBS in Boston for twenty-five years. His rare counterparts can usually be found in the state of Vermont. Smells vaguely of carpeting. Always speaks in a hushed tone, as if he were being closely miked, except when he discusses his favorite topics, which include dietary roughage, ventilation (never enough of either), pensions, and "institutions" that "have blown it all to shit" and "should take more cues from the BBC," which is The Peeb's equivalent of Narnia. Rides a Raleigh three-speed to work, using a set of elaborate hand signals alien to 99 percent of drivers, with an ancient leather brief-case strapped to his back, and pant protectors encircling pockmarked brown cords. Sometimes gets a lift from his wife (beige '88 Volvo) — a former student from the year he taught journalism at Boston University and mother to his only child (born when The Peeb was fifty). Has been developing a television version of NPR's *Fresh Air* program for two decades. Recently was "retrained" as a technical-editorial "hybrid" and found himself working on a "multicultural morning-show concept." His boss is a beautiful Sri Lankan spitfire half his age whom he detests as much as he does those who park their bikes too close to his at the stand (he has contacted the union), but possibly not as much as those who "mismanage" the co-op (there is a real issue with the food bins) near his South End home (bought for a song in 1983 — recently paid off with an inheritance). Says he is not "bitter," just "abused by the atrophying system." Dreams of setting up a bed and breakfast in Cape Cod.

VICTORIANNA

AVERAGE AGE: 48
NATURAL HABITAT: Ye Olde Christmas Shoppe

VictoriAnna is a fan of anything that is commonly referred to as "period" in popular culture, as in "period movie" or "period home." Some VictoriAnnas are of the all-in variety, and others are devoted to a specific era in history. The oddest by far are those who favor the medieval years, and the most irritating are the ones partial to the gilded age, who try to re-create Dorothy Parker's Vicious Circle with martini glasses purchased at Pier 1 Imports. The most common VictoriAnna is often found in New York State or New England. Fond of quilts, worm-eaten wood, and anything "olde fashioned." VictoriAnnas like "throw" anything (rugs, cushions, blankets), pot-pourri sachets, and those stores that sell fancy Christmas ornaments all year round. They might keep VHS tapes or DVDs in boxes that look like the outside of leather-bound books. Six out of ten VictoriAnnas sleep in those white cotton full-length nighties that numerous women seem to find "sexy in a pure kind of way" and no men find sexy in any way. Obviously, VictoriAnnas are movie-going hell for most of their male mates or husbands, men who will try tricks like "But *King Kong* IS a period movie."

THE STEWARTITE

AVERAGE AGE: 32
NATURAL HABITAT: Watching *The Daily Show*

A devotee of *The Daily Show*'s Jon Stewart, The Stewartite has joined The Seinfeldiot and *The Simpsons* Quoter as among the most ubiquitous animals in the TV-fan subset. The nerdiest of this nerds-who-don't-think-they-are-nerds species might wear a "Take that, Tucker!" T-shirt, an allusion to the CNN *Crossfire* segment ("a show, by the way, which has been *canceled*," The Stewartite reminds us) in which Stewart asked the insufferable Tucker Carlson to "stop, stop, stop hurting America" with "partisan hackery." A typical Stewartite might hold a job he considers far beneath his intellectual abilities and "political savoir faire." ("You know, I read *Time* AND *Newsweek* every week AND *The Atlantic* every month. I'm just saying.") He may even think of himself as "subversive." He also considers the Dave Matthews Band (his favorite) "subversive." Muses daily (and possibly on a blog) about whether Stewart's protégé, Stephen Colbert, has "surpassed the master." Tends to classify events or issues as either a "-gate" (Marthagate, Enrongate) or a "-stock" (Bushstock, Kerrystock). Thinks anyone who does not find Stewart and his "Who, me?" face-mugging funny either "doesn't get it" or, if the naysayer is a media personality or politician, is "tied to a White House conspiracy." Actually owns a DVD of the notable 2002 flop *Death to Smoochy*, in which Stewart is a featured actor. It goes without saying that The Stewartite is a serial quoter of his television deity. Favorite lines include "Ahh, Earth Day — the only day of the year when being able to hacky sack will get you laid." "It's funny," says The Stewartite, a die-hard hacky sacker, "because it's so true."

THE YURY

AVERAGE AGE: 32
NATURAL HABITAT: The cottage

The Yury is the Young Urban Ruralist. When she was a child, her parents had a country house — they called it a "cottage" even though it had six bedrooms and something called a "hot rock sauna" — but after the age of fourteen, she refused to "give up weekends to skiing" when she could throw totally tubular parties in her parents' gilded manse in the city. Now an adult and "tired of the rat race and the scene," she has discovered that she "actually loves the country." She finds this very satisfying — proof, even more than yoga, that she is a "soulful being." After eight years of "working in the media," she has bought her own place "up north" instead of "some loft in the city" and "feels a great sense of wellness" when she packs up her SUV (warranted — all those country roads) with groceries from Whole Foods for the weekends. Has taken to cooking her guests "country dishes" featuring ham hocks. (And there must be guests, for if there are no guests, no one can see how *relaxed* The Yury is by the fire, in her cashmere Juicy Couture sweat pants.) After dinners, forces guests to sit around drinking red wine even if they want to go to sleep. This is to best replicate that "warm camaraderie" one sometimes sees in "those French movies where friends sit around in a country house and have real *intellectual* discussion until dawn." After last week's feast (ham with ham hock–simmered beans), she urged her guests to "gather around the hearth — anyone for some *brandy?*" but one guest turned on the TV, and they all ended up watching *Mad TV*, which made The Yury very perturbed, because watching *Mad TV* is incredibly un-countrylike. Says that "everybody" is buying houses in the country now (secretly feels like she "started the trend"), and not in "the gentrified" part, where her parents had their place, but "*real* country — it's not just weekenders around these parts." Is fond of saying she "lives near people who put on Kodiaks to go to work." But not too near, of course.

THE FRIENDSTER

AVERAGE AGE: 30
NATURAL HABITAT: Evidently, all

The Friendster spent last Saturday night in a bar drinking with a butcher who had just emigrated from Moscow. The Friendster's actual date had to cancel at the last second, but, by the time she'd reached The Friendster's phone, he'd already made a new buddy in Vladimir. Flash friendships such as this one are normal for The Friendster, who, though he looks completely unassuming, forgettable even, has a knack for picking up people — often odd ones — as if they were coins on the street. He always has a collection of novel pals he's very excited about — people whose acquaintance he has made while waiting for the subway, shopping in the supermarket, or standing in line for a bank machine. His travel stories are legendary: the one where he ended up on the Greek shipping billionaire's yacht; the one where he subbed as a DP on an X-rated film shoot in an Orlando motel. His friend Charlie once accused The Friendster of having "a compulsive need for new human material." But this is only half right. "It's weird," says The Friendster's younger brother, Zack, "people just come up to him — like he's got some huge neon welcome mat hanging on his forehead." Zack once asked his brother what the magnetic trick is. "I dunno," said The Friendster. "Maybe it's something in my eyes. I keep them bright." "Right," said Zack. "Bright eyes." Zack spent the rest of that day with his eyeballs almost popping out of their sockets. A woman sitting across from him at Starbucks asked if he was ill. Zack called his brother's cell. "The eyes — it's not really working," he said. "Never mind! Come meet me," replied The Friendster. "I just met the head of the United Steelworkers union, and he's invited me to their annual Bowl-a-Thon. It's going to be *a blast*."